SLIDE COLLECTION MANAGEMENT IN LIBRARIES AND INFORMATION UNITS

Slide Collection Management in Libraries and Information Units

Glyn Sutcliffe

Gower

Published by
Gower Publishing Limited
Gower House
Croft Road
Aldershot
Hampshire GU11 3HR
England

Gower
Old Post Road
Brookfield
Vermont 05036
USA

G. Sutcliffe has asserted his right under the Copyright, Designs and Patents Act 1988 to be identified as the author of this work.

British Library Cataloguing in Publication Data

Sutcliffe, Glyn
  Slide Collection Management in Libraries
  and Information Units
  I. Title
  025. 1773

ISBN 0–566–07580–6

Library of Congress Cataloging-in-Publication Data

Sutcliffe, Glyn.
  Slide collection management in libraries and information units /
Glyn Sutcliffe.
    p.   cm.
  Includes bibliographical references (p.) and index.
  ISBN 0–566–07580–6
  1. Libraries—Great Britain—Special collections—Slides
(Photography)   I. Title.
Z692.S65S87 1995   94—22678
025.3'47—dc20   CIP

Typeset in Palatino by Raven Typesetters, Chester and printed
in Great Britain by Hartnolls Ltd, Bodwin

Contents

Appendices:

List of tables and figures

Acknowledgements

I would like to particularly thank Mr Phil Muse of Calderdale College Electronic Media Unit for information and advice relating to the material on new imaging systems.

Thanks are also due to the staffs of the following libraries: Calderdale College Library; Leeds Metropolitan University Library; The Information and Library Studies Library of the Department of Information and Library Studies, University of Wales, Aberystwyth.

I am also grateful to the representatives of the many organizations listed in the Appendices, both in the UK and the USA, who all generously contributed valuable time, expertise and information.

Acknowledgements

Preface

Continuing advances in the generation of computer graphics, the capacity of compact disc storage and the quality of high definition television and computer monitors are destined to give new significance to pictorial information and its uses in society, to image data systems and picture libraries. The ability of the new technologies to store, manipulate and retrieve images of all types, with increasing speed, is creating new standards and new expectations of service in the retrieval and use of images.

The quality of the electronically created and stored images, though not yet perfected technically or fully established in the market-place, is shortly set to equal or surpass that of the established methods of picture reproduction.

Far from diminishing the value of the vast resources contained in existing picture collections and libraries of all types, the development of automated methods of image information management are likely to make established picture collections, whose holdings include a wide variety of picture and photographic formats, of enhanced value and importance.

Within this wider context the 35mm photographic slide holds a secure if somewhat unacclaimed position. The ease with which high quality images can be created in the slide format and the familiarity of the medium to most people has led to a continuing accumulation of collections in a host of subject fields and academic disciplines over a lengthy period. The subsequent practices used to manage these collections by both amateurs and information professionals are almost as diverse as the subject matter of the material, although a measure of unity is evident in clearly defined subject areas.

It is difficult and perhaps unwise to forecast how the existing, well-established, conventional slide collections will be changed by developments in electronic picture creation and storage. At one extreme there is the threat that conventional photography could be rendered obsolete and, at the other, the possibility of slides being generated from electronic storage on such a massive scale that the result will be a corresponding expansion in slide collections.

Whatever the future holds, it is an appropriate time to review how slide collections have developed, particularly in the subject fields where collections are extensive, identifiable and have been fulfilling clear user requirements for many years.

Looking back from the inception of the lantern slide to the present, there is a worthy history of those charged with the care of slide collections providing services, using manual methods, often under difficult circumstances and with scarce resources. The valuable building work carried out during this period forms a rich heritage particularly with regard to the unique material accumulated and to a lesser extent in information management terms.

Looking forwards there is every cause for optimism for the slide to realize more of its potential as a source of pictorial information, principally through the power of access made possible by automated retrieval systems.

Furthermore, the advances being made in the innovative application of computer and video technology to control and provide greater subject access to the illusive nature of pictorial information, has created a new momentum and urgency to reassess the value of slides and their place within libraries and information units.

While not fulfilling the role of a definitive manual of practice, it is hoped that this work goes some way to forging closer links between the disparate fields which use slides, and will further the work of students, be beneficial to practising slide managers and prove of value to future researchers.

Glyn Sutcliffe

1   Background and trends in slide collection management

Introduction

A picture is a visual information item and a positive transparent photographic image or slide is merely one format in which a picture may be presented. A variety of sizes of transparency exist and are important in a number of differing working situations. The larger formats of full plate – 8.5 × 6.5 inch, 5 × 4 inch and 2.25 inch square are favoured wherever quality reproduction is paramount. The larger original image size allows for a lesser degree of enlargement, does not reveal the inherent grain structure of the image and thus produces a clearer finished print. As a result these sizes are used for reproduction in magazines and quality journals. However, the modern, much smaller, 35mm slide abounds in almost all fields and is a unique format within the world of pictures and more particularly in libraries where the format is of an optimum size for lending and projection. The 35mm format is known as the 'miniature slide' having evolved from the substantially larger lantern slide and also being diminutive in comparison with other modern transparency formats.

The format has many merits, both as an item in the management of pictorial information, and for the communication and information purposes of picture users which make it worthy of consideration for inclusion in almost any library collection, whether that be alongside other print and non-print formats or to stand alone to form a separate collection.

The retrieval of pictures

Almost all libraries have requests for pictorial representations of objects, people, places etc. Often such enquiries are answered from encyclopedias and other illustrated print sources. An admirable description of the problems encountered in this area is given by Lee, where the illusive nature of visual enquiry work is clearly conveyed and the few sources of assistance which do exist are well covered.[1]

The search for illustrative matter in this way has to be carried out through retrieval systems established for print material and relies heavily on the librarian's professionally developed expertise and familiarity with appropriate books which are known to include pictorial material. Quite often a likely source does not include the specific illustration requested and such searches, therefore, sometimes involve more than a small amount of intuition. As Lee states, 'The librarian can often hope only that what appears to be a promising book does have the pictures he requires.'[2]

In this context a separately administered and suitably indexed picture collection is invaluable in reducing the intuitive element when conducting picture searches. Such a collection need not necessarily be composed entirely of slides, but it will be argued here that slides provide a compact and serviceable bank of pictorial information at affordable cost which will more than repay the outlay in terms of information provision. Naturally, printed pictures will always be important to certain categories of library user, but for many libraries where pictorial information may or may not be their primary concern, slides represent a wise choice when wishing to establish an effective working collection, whether it is for reference work as just referred to or for lending purposes. Methods of rapidly producing prints from slides are now available for those users for whom a transparency is inappropriate.

The problems associated with quickly and conveniently obtaining illustrative material particularly for publication or re-publication in specialized areas is the reason for the profession of picture researcher. Such personnel owe their working existence to the illusive nature of images and to the labour required to obtain images for a precisely defined need. Although slides have a part to play in this process, since most publishers favour reprocessing from transparency material, it is usually the larger formats which are demanded rather than 35mm. Nevertheless the structure of the profession of picture researcher, the Society of Picture Researchers and Editors (SPRed) and the related literature provides another area of activity relevant to slide libraries.

Many commercial picture libraries are affiliated to the British Association of Picture Libraries and Agencies (BAPLA). This trade association has done much co-ordinating work in the supply and licensing of pictures for reproduction and in advising photographers on contracts, legal representation, copyright and other working problems. The Association expects members to abide by a professional code of conduct and regulates professional standards of the membership. The BAPLA journal and the BAPLA directory are both respected and invaluable publications in an important sector of commercial picture activity which has growing direct links with academic, educational or other non-commercial picture libraries. Increasingly institutions such as museums are developing their commercially run services in exploiting the materials they hold.[3]

The slide and the establishment of slide collections permeate many more areas of activity than simply the academic and educational visual art field. This is due to the slide's particular advantages as an image format.

The merits of the slide
The following list covers a number of the slide's characteristics as a format which make it of value in the above mentioned connections and in libraries and information centres in general.

1   It is relatively easy to quickly accumulate a sizeable collection of slides at moderate cost. In addition to acquisition from commercial sources, collections in most library situations can be expanded rapidly from in-house sources and, in many cases, unique and valuable collections have been established from sources within the same organization which the collection serves.

2   A collection can be stored in a compact space and in a secure way and with normal usage does not necessarily require many staff-hours to maintain. (It has to be acknowledged, however, that the relevant specialist skills need to be developed at the outset and conversion work can require a lot of attention when collections are being established or management methods changed.)

3   The individual images can be rearranged from their order in storage and composed according to the user's individual requirements to make up a unique, custom-made lecture support package. Furthermore, quick access, browsing and comparison of the positive images is more convenient than it is for the larger picture formats or photographic negatives.

4   The flexibility of sequential arrangement makes the slide ideal for meeting the individual personal needs of users. The size and clarity of the projected picture enables the same message to reach all in a numerous audience simultaneously, yet remain in parallel with the verbal message delivered by the teacher, lecturer or instructor. In addition the projected picture size can be infinitely and readily adjusted to audience numbers, a unique advantage in the lecturing/teaching situation.

5   The cost of accompanying hardware (projectors) is comparatively low, compared with, for example, video disc projection equipment or large screen video. Also the manageability, transportability and usual availability of such equipment at teaching or lecturing venues again favours slide usage.

6 In purely technical terms the need for transmitted light to create the projected image leads to a brighter image and to a greater contrast range than a picture viewed by reflected light or the television picture. In some respects the slide image can even be said, in some instances, to be an improvement on the original subject of the illustration or its lighting. Indeed it has been noted that art students have been disappointed at the lack of luminance of originals after being introduced to works initially only through their representation on a slide.

The only other formats dependent on transmitted light to achieve a bright image are stained glass or painting directly onto a glass or other transparent surface. Although stained glass has not asserted itself as a library format in this world it could perhaps be seen as having some potential for the next!

Awareness of the slide as an item in library collections

Despite the above and the fact that the 35mm colour slide is over 50 years old, the format remains somewhat submerged and unacclaimed in the information world as a whole. As a consequence the slide has never realized its full potential in as many fields as it perhaps could have, or been widely or enthusiastically adopted and promoted in all libraries or other information units. The majority of the reported work which has been done on slide management is in the visual arts and architecture fields and to a lesser extent in the area of medical teaching/records and construction industry libraries. Added to this there is the natural associated interest inherent in the broad studies of picture librarianship and audio-visual librarianship. Although large collections of pictorial material are held by commercial picture collections and press and picture agencies there appears to be no substantial reports of how these collections are managed in practice or could be managed in theory.

Other areas of slide usage which often remain somewhat overlooked are those within public libraries, archives and museums. Photographic surveys and local historical collections, possibly including lantern slides, are in many cases only known to those in charge of the accumulation and care of the collections and probably to a limited number of local users. Collections of this type can remain unpublicized to a wider clientele and also to information professionals wishing to point prospective users in the right direction. The lack of sources making known the existence and extent of slide collections is not attributable to the shortcomings or negligence of any individual or professional group, but does indicate how slide collections have been bypassed and remained largely unresearched as a national information resource for almost the whole of the time of their growth and development. Certain directories of various ages give patchy coverage and a variety of detail on the size and subject scope of collections. While they collectively give indications of the existence of many slide resources, they are inadequate in providing an up-to-date national profile of slide collections with sufficient detail on which to base further research or confident conclusions.[4] The modern 35mm slide appeared in the mid-1930s and a number of collections date from then, but the main expansion in the size and number of collections came with the boom years of the 1960s when educational establishments and libraries prospered economically. During this developmental period indications are that substantial collections were established in a wide variety of institutions. As will be covered in more detail shortly, initial research has been completed into comprehensively listing slide collections and their holdings on a national basis and in making their existence a matter of public record.

Problems of the slide as a library item
While the slide has the advantages and potentialities mentioned above it cannot be ignored that it also has some inconveniences or problems as a library format which require careful consideration by custodians.

The individual slide is a small and somewhat fragile item. The photographic emulsion is vulnerable to scratching, atmospheric attack and damage during normal handling and from the high temperatures of projection. Natural ageing processes can also change the colours of the dyes or virtually eliminate one colour entirely. Appreciable improvements have been made in this respect and modern slides are much more stable and the base materials stronger than earlier slides.

Further to these technical shortcomings, the slide as a library item and particularly as a loan item can be easily lost. A single slide can appear insignificant and if detached from a body of other slides can be easily misplaced and forgotten. Fifty slides borrowed, 49 slides returned, result: misery! – especially for future borrowers and for the long-term future of the affected collection. The conventional library recovery system of overdue notices, fines or invoices is unlikely to be vigorously invoked to secure the return of a single slide under such circumstances, since the costs of doing so could not be recovered or justified. In this way all slide collections are vulnerable, over the years, to a cumulative, stealthy erosion which can insidiously reduce their coverage.

Another difficulty stemming from the slide's small size is that it affords little space on which to identify the library to which it belongs. The space is more likely to be taken up by the description of the illustration, the class mark or, possibly, in the art library what is termed 'the attribution', the provenance and functional origin details. Any lack of identity can contribute to slides going astray or being returned to the wrong library or other such confusions.

Problems of retrieval and circulation
In general terms the establishment of effective retrieval systems and loan records, which are cost effective and efficient for the staff available, are not simple matters for slide managers who are dealing with collections made up of, and designed to exploit, individual images. The problems of circulation systems are simplified if the collection is composed of sets or predetermined fixed sequences of slides which can be issued as separate packaged entities. Much work remains to be done in devising efficient slide issuing systems, but at present the problems remain intractable. Methods such as photocopying borrowers' records together with the details of the slides borrowed have been tried with some local success. However, the likely future answer to the difficulties of recording accurately the large quantity of detailed

information, when a number of slides are issued, is the development of existing automated systems to cover this important service feature of slide libraries. Where much data are already held for automated cataloguing purposes it is logical to use this data for issue as well as retrieval purposes. The use of bar code labels to quickly access stored data and to record issues appears to be the probable direction of advances, and indications are that this is the case. In this way both retrieval and circulation will be covered in comprehensive management systems controlling the movements of the slides as well as descriptive and indexing information about them. This will lead to the reduction of some of the laborious routine manual procedures which slide library staff have to undertake.

Furthermore, with respect to retrieval, although valiant attempts have been made to use manual methods to control and provide access to slide collections by the use of visual indexes, on 5 × 3 inch cards for example, the return on the labour involved at the input stage can make the effort uneconomic.[5] This is particularly so when automated alternatives are available. Manual methods of retrieval – typed lists, card catalogues or self-indexed collections where cards are interfiled with the slides – can only offer a limited number of approaches to the material. It is only with the advent of microcomputers and database management systems at affordable prices that the data handling involved in slide management can be, or has been, reduced to manageable proportions and a more comprehensive range of approaches provided which cater for the large majority of users' needs. The manual retrieval methods devised over the years from about 1960–85, in many cases were ingenious and laudable, but the reality was that the return on the intensive labour at the input stage was not well rewarded at the output stage where user needs as always were many and various. By contrast the investment in an automated system produces so many more approaches to the pictorial information that could not be provided for by manual methods because of the amount of labour, both clerical and professional, that is involved. For these reasons the significance of the ability of computing power to enable slide collections to be liberated from the limitations of manual retrieval systems and realize their true value, can hardly be over-estimated.

The value of applying automated management methods

It is almost as though the true beginning for slide library exploitation is in reality now, and that the history of collections has simply been a preliminary period of stock development prior to a way being found to unlock the considerable resources and provide multiple access routes to the slides accumulated over previous decades. The time is now at hand when the automated management of slide collections is a prerequisite rather than a luxury or optional extra. If this appears something of an overstatement there is no doubt that the progressive reduction of the unit costs of computing power, in real terms, has led to a situation where in the future it will be the exception for any medium or large slide collection to be managed using a manual system.

Interrelationship of the slide with other advanced picture- making technology

Technological advances in other directions also have implications for the future of slide collections. For example, the continued improvement of the resolution of the television picture and of computer graphics and the development of video tape, video disc, the filmless camera and visuals stored on CD-ROM has ensured a growing, a continuing and, in some quarters, a renewed interest in the importance of pictorial information and image collections. These are located in various areas of information communication and storage including news gathering, education and training, surveillance and record-keeping in many fields. The quest for a high resolution electronically-produced picture has concentrated attention on the constituent elements of such pictures, namely the television picture scanning-lines or in computer terms the pixel.

Re-evaluation of the visual image and progressing work trends on slides in libraries

New electronic picture-making methods have naturally led to a re-evaluation of the visual image in technological terms. Clark calculates that a television picture is worth about 100,000 words rather than the proverbial 1,000.[6] No doubt a photographic slide image with its considerably greater resolution is worth many more. Indeed, the picture quality of a slide is of such a high standard that it is perhaps difficult for the slide user to be conscious that the resultant picture is made up of dots or has any grain, as all photographic images, of necessity, possess. Despite fierce competition from technological progress in picture making, slide collections do not seem set to be made immediately obsolete, but with the successful application of computers to their management, do appear to be well placed to develop further and become important sources of pictorial material complementing the pictures generated by other means by the new technologies.

In any event there is no doubt that information technology and computing methods are continuing to have an increasingly strong and pervasive influence on the way information in all its forms is managed in libraries. This effect, as Clark above suggests, involves in part, searching for the smallest constituent part of pictorial information and from there progressing to an understanding of how these elements combine and eventually build up to form a recognizable or interpretable message for sensory perception.

Also, again, as mentioned above, the development of electronically-generated pictures has suggested new ways of conceptualizing the make up of images, but it would appear that the slide is well placed to compete strongly with the newer picture carrying media in the immediate and medium term future and retain its popularity with existing users.

The above consideration of the equivalence of words and pictures or, perhaps more accurately, the relationship between written and graphic information, and how this affects our view of the true nature of pictorial information, and access to individual images in collections of pictures, is fundamental to advancement in the understanding of how picture and slide collections can best be managed in their entirety and, more particularly, how retrieval systems can best be operated.

More specifically for the purposes of this book, the treatment of slide resources in library collections is part of this wider concern and it is an issue which will be resolved rather more by the evolution of a consensus of practice within libraries over an indeterminate time period than by pronouncements by an individual author making subjective judgements (however well informed!). There are indications though, that there is a movement within libraries and by information professionals to re-evaluate the place of slide resources in professionally structured collections and co-ordinate the various strands of work which have evolved over the many years that slides have been incorporated in library collections in diverse ways.

Libraries concerned with the fine arts and the history of art and architecture have always been at the forefront of picture librarianship and in the development of slide collections because of their own and their parent institutions' inherent interest in the aesthetic and artistic qualities of light and pictorial representations of all kinds.

The Art Libraries Society of the United Kingdom (ARLIS/UK and Ireland) has in recent years been a focus for the co-ordination of art slide curators' interest in slides through newsletter items and 'Slide Forums' or meetings to exchange ideas and discuss ways of advancing knowledge and awareness of slide management methods. Such liaisons were instrumental or a strong contributing factor in bringing about the British Library research project leading to the compilation of the *National directory of slide collections* (McKeown, 1990)[7] and in providing a platform for, and highlighting, the need to establish a recognized professional status for slide managers.[8] The wide variety of situational position of many slide managers and their differing educational and training backgrounds does not make this an easy problem to solve. The fact that not all slide managers, by any means, have had a professional training in librarianship perhaps makes it more necessary that some formal recognition or identity is created to give coherent unity to a body of people undoubtedly sharing a common professional occupation and often educated to graduate level. The need to develop both subject knowledge and expertise in information work is a point well made by the Visual Resources Association during its establishment and development.

The initiative to produce the *National directory* was an example of the interest in slides in one subject discipline being a starting point for a project which had the wider brief of including details of collections from as many other fields as possible. Such developments are indicative of a timely expansion of activity in gathering basic information on slide collections and beginning to form a basis for co-ordinating slide collection management activities across disciplines or collections in different subject areas.

Although there is a corresponding interest and activity concerning slides in the medical field there is as yet no significant dialogue between those working with collections in the arts field and those in the medical. To many the suggestion that this should take place would seem out of place or inappropriate. The Institute of Medical and Biological Illustration (IMBI) is the main professional body through which those working in the field of medical photography exchange knowledge, experiences and ideas. However, the Institute's members are drawn almost exclusively from medical photographers and those employed in departments of medical illustration within hospitals and ties are not well established with medical libraries or the Library Association or, indeed, any part of the formally constituted information community.

In the museums field the Museums Documentation Association (MDA) exists to establish standards of documentation in museums throughout the UK. Naturally the main concern is for the management of museum exhibits, but this embraces or extends in no small way to images of all kinds. The close cultural and administrative association of museums with art galleries provides strong links with the fine arts world. Slides can exist in museums either as exhibits (usually lantern slides) or as educational support materials for staff talks, exhibitions or other educational activities. Developments in visual arts libraries such as the publication of *Art and Architecture Thesaurus (AAT)* have applications in museum standards. Although no directory comprehensively documents the extent of slide collections in museums they do indicate that they are present and with the significance of images in museums it is safe to assume that moderate numbers are extant.

The MDA is involved with advice and the adoption of automated systems for museum documentation. The MODES cataloguing system can be used for photographic collections and thus applied to slides. The increasing prominence and wider adoption of ICONCLASS, the iconographic classification system, is also relevant in a wider context than museums although the scheme is routed in the Western art history field.

In the US the greater development of museum libraries as a clearly identifiable library subject group has naturally led to more contributions to the literature of slide management in this context.

Preconceptions concerning slides
Moreover, within the library community slides suffer, as do audio-visual materials, in general, from a lingering legacy of preconceptions fostered by tradition and a solid stability which prevailed over a long period. The traditionally close identification or near equivalence of the terms book and library established over so many centuries has quite naturally taken a considerable time to be revised in many people's minds to accommodate the inclusion of other information-carrying formats. The uncritical acceptance of the traditional relationship over many years, to some extent by librarians and by library users, led to other information-carrying formats being packaged in ways which give the outward appearance of books in order that they could be incorporated conveniently in classified sequences of books and conform not only to existing subject shelf arrangements, but to almost everyone's idea of what packaged information should look like. Clearly, the historical evolution of libraries has, in the past, created something of a 'strait-jacket' of thought towards information in formats other than the book. This rigid outlook is only beginning to be loosened in comparatively recent times. Such liberation requires a return to first principles and to initially exclude the preconceptions of dealing with all information from the stereotyped position created by, or inherited from, methods of dealing with systematic collections of the book. Many well-established slide collections are managed by personnel who do not possess formal professional library training. While on the

negative side such people may not have as wide an appreciation of the information world as the professional librarian, in positive terms they will not possess the preconceptions which a professional librarian is likely to have towards slides when almost certainly approaching their management from a background of managing print based collections. The 'non-librarian' will, therefore, be able to bring an unprejudiced and more impartial approach to the difficulties of slide management and this freshness of thought should not be underestimated when considering the totality of slide management in structured collections.

Further considerations concerning the integration or segregation of AV material and slides

The packaging of tape/slide sequences and video tapes in libraries, for example, has been developed to the extent that gold lettered 'spines' on boxes have been employed to simulate a book appearance. Such procrustean methods can only be justified by the help this affords to the user who, when conducting a subject search, has only one (or as few as possible) sequences of materials to check. However, when library users make requests for information they often specify the format in which it is required. They do this as a condition which can precede their actual subject requirement and which in the process knowingly rejects information in other formats. For example, a person requiring a recording of a symphony is unlikely to be satisfied with the score of that symphony and is also likely to be dissatisfied with a video recording of a performance when simply demanding an audio version. Clearly, such an argument is not diminished when requests for pictorial material are made. Often a particular pictorial format is required by a user and no substitute is satisfactory.

For these reasons and because many AV media cannot be easily browsed through on the shelf, separate sequences of materials by format are a logical and often preferred alternative to complete subject integration on the shelves. In the case of sequences of slides, either in tape/slide programmes or slide sets of varying numbers, the packages can be either integrated in a subject sequence with other or all of a library's stock or stored separately by format as preferred. However, the collection of individual slides, though possibly closely related to one subject theme, dictates by its very physical composition that it must be segregated from other library materials and demands separate specialist management to be fully exploited.

The need for libraries to index their collections to make them accessible to users, has generated an extensive literature relating to the retrieval of textual information. In some instances the techniques thus developed have been directly applied to the retrieval of pictorial material. Often, however, the significance of an illustration lies more with the viewer and their uses of the illustration than with its creator. For example, a picture user may be interested in something within or which is a minor part of, and is incidental to the main subject of an illustration. Such a significance cannot be foreseen by the originator of the picture and can demand almost clairvoyant qualities on the part of the indexer who is concerned with finding probable, likely or potential uses of the illustration when assigning indexing terms. The passage of time may also alter the significance of the content of a picture for those who are concerned with its end use: both slide collection manager and borrower. Whereas the significance of a body of writing lies with its creator and it is the author who effectively engenders the indexing terms which are implicit in the composition, this is not the case with pictorial material where indexing terms may have to reflect likely uses.

Although when considering some of the complexities of the retrieval of print and of pictorial information, it is perhaps true to say that the indexing of print material is not beset by this same imponderable problem as outlined above. In the case of print material the probable uses and significant aspects are implicit within the body of writing and the end uses are far less likely to vary quite in the way the use of pictorial information can. Another key, if rather obvious, difference is that when indexing print materials the common medium of language is being used for the indexed item and the indexing language whereas the indexing of illustrations requires a translation of the indexable facets of the illustration into the words of an indexing language.

As Clark states in this connection,

Pictures are rich in ambiguities of all sorts. Indeed, these ambiguities are the very essence of images; they offer the multiplicity of associations and entry points that so facilitate comprehension. Nevertheless, a collection of pictures is a database, but how can such a database of images be searched?[9]

and as Harrison states, 'a picture's ability to communicate information which cannot be expressed in words is of unique value.'[10]

If it is accepted that television and other media influences have ensured that we now live in a picture dominated environment and society, it is perhaps surprising that greater attention has not been paid to the development and unification of practices surrounding the management of slide collections. The principal reasons for this lack of concentrated attention on the slide is possibly the way in which the format has evolved historically, both photographically and in systematically organized collections, and the way in which slide collections have always had strong specialized subject associations. This has resulted in those in different fields pursuing independent courses and methods of management. 'It appears that each field of endeavour has attempted to organise its slides according to its own unique requirements.'[11]

The evolution of the slide and slide collections
The outline chronology of the development of the slide and slide collections is:

1830s	Invention of photography.
1841	Introduction of the glass slide.
1840–80	Natural accumulation of glass slides by photographers, patrons etc.
1861	Invention of celluloid.
1880s	First mention of academic glass slide collections in US.
1884	Roll film system patented by George Eastman.
1880–1940s	Substantial collections of glass slides accumulated in visual arts fields.
1891	Introduction of first 35mm cine film.

1914	Oskar Barnack, optical designer for microscope manufacturers Ernst Leitz, produces prototype of Leica 35mm camera – first 35mm still camera.
	Commercial production delayed by First World War and its aftermath.
1924	Leica 35mm camera available commercially.
1930s	Other competing 35mm cameras produced – Zeiss-Ikon Contax (1932), Kodak Retina (1934) and Agfa Karat (1937).
1930s	Kodachrome three colour process patented and creation of modern 35mm or 2×2 inch mounted slide as known today.
1930s–60s	Establishment and steady growth of collections of modern 35mm slides in a variety of fields, alongside other picture formats in art libraries in particular, but also as independent collections in other fields, e.g. medical teaching.
1960s–present	Technical advances in stability of base material for film and in permanence of dyes used in film emulsion.
1984–present	Competition for the slide from new electronically generated picture technologies from video tape, video disc, compact disc and computer graphics.
	But, also, new demands made on slide collections to supply the need for illustrations created by the new technology and general interaction in the picture-making market-place.

Although multidisciplinary collections, or collections of slides covering a number of related fields, do exist as picture resource banks it is far more often the case that collections are centred on a single discipline and serve a clearly defined user group. In general terms this is usually an academic or commercially involved clientele with specific requirements. The main areas referred to here are the fine arts, architecture, medicine, and building enterprises where slides are most prominent, but slide collections exist in a wide variety of other situations. The list below covers the majority of these.

Furthermore, slides are to be found alongside other information materials in libraries or information units, but equally they exist as 'stand alone' collections meeting specialized needs. More specifically with respect to picture libraries slide collections are in many cases allied to and supporting picture stocks of prints, negatives and other picture formats, but quite often they can be the only picture format held by a library. This almost endless variety in the combination of circumstance and situation extends to staffing expertise and levels, the financing of collections and size and nature of the user groups.

The survey of picture libraries by Coulson provides a concise summary of the situation of which slides form a part.[12] Coulson provides a useful categorization of picture library by function: archival; commercial; teaching and private research. Although slides or slide libraries can be regarded as a subsection of picture libraries, as previously noted, slide collections can exist in isolation from other picture formats and thus in this sense extend outside the area of general picture collections.

The following list indicates where slide collections can be found. Although there is a certain degree of cross classification (for example medical collections are also academic) this is deliberate in order to indicate the variety of location and subject.

Classified list of slide holding organizations
National
National libraries
National museums
National archives

Visual Arts
Art galleries
Art libraries

Medical   Departments of medical illustration and to a lesser extent medical libraries in:

Teaching hospitals
Regional hospitals
Postgraduate medical centres
Schools/Colleges of Nursing

Academic
Institutes of Higher Education
Colleges
Universities

Public
Public libraries
Archives
Public record offices
Museums

National government and government supported
Government departments
Research institutes
Research associations

Local authorities
Local authority departments

Industry/business
Large industrial concerns
Architectural practices
Construction firms

Media
Television companies
Newspapers
Commercial picture libraries
Picture agencies
Press agencies
Advertising agencies
Publishing houses
Journals
Freelance/professional photographers

Services
Water
Gas
Electricity
Nuclear Fuels

Social/personal
Individual amateur photographers
Private individuals
Specialist interest clubs

Other
Learned societies
Professional associations
Tourist boards and centres
Charities
Pressure groups

Although a space has long existed in the UK literature concerned with slide management, it is only relatively recently that it has been detectable that there is a growing awareness in the wider-information community of the value of efficiently run slide libraries. There is an appreciation of the worth of slide collections which have status within existing libraries or as separately managed collections rather than haphazard, idly accumulated 'shoe box' slide collections which are, or have a tendency to become, an embarrassment to both staff and users.

These are a number of the wide range of issues and influences which surround the continuing development of slide collections and slides in libraries. It may be that slide librarianship will be a long time in emerging as a clearly discernable aspect of librarianship as such with a discreet identity and demarcation as to its limits. The area may remain a hybrid field of activity which while being well represented in professionally managed libraries, nevertheless extends into other areas with moderate, little or no obvious allegiance or link with the wider information community. The different fields where slide collections have developed may well continue to pursue essentially independent courses. Be that as it may, this is an appropriate time for a state-ment of the present development of slide management and for a co-ordinating contribution in a fragmented area of information work which is likely to benefit from a sharper profile and an exchange and pooling of the expertise which exists in many dif-ferent, but loosely related areas.

The time *is* especially appropriate because of:

1   the increasing availability and use of automation imposes a greater discipline and consistency when compiling data and the overall influence of computer methods is to offer the opportunity for more standardized practices being adopted in slide collection management.

2   competition for the slide from other image producing tech-nologies such as filmless cameras, video disc, computer graphics, high resolution television, video tape and perhaps most significantly CD, make it necessary to be clear about the value of slide collections and what they can still uniquely offer in the face of the competition.

It has been suggested that new picture producing technology will overtake the slide and render it obsolete,[13] but such con-clusions are premature and the slide retains some unique characteristics, especially in the teaching situation, which have not as yet been emulated by electronically-produced picture formats.

3   how organized slide resources can contribute to picture usage in conjunction with the new electronic picture produc-ing methods by supplying still pictures from existing slide resources through the process known as frame capture.

4   the desire of those working with slides to receive recognition and develop a professional identity not only for their own advancement, but for the sake also of their clientele, the ser-vice they provide and the betterment of slide collections.

In view of the factors touched on above it is necessary to set out some working definitions to simply provide a starting point and to clarify the terms involved. Slide collections exist in a wide variety of subject fields. They are managed in library terms by a wide variety of methods and by personnel from numerous different professional and technical backgrounds, but useful comparisons can be drawn, similarities pointed out and possibly some useful common methods clarified.

Of necessity all systematically structured slide collections share the need to control their stock for acquisition and circulation, provide adequate retrieval devices and meet the demands of a user group. They also share the characteristics of any library to collect, store, retrieve and exploit the materials to the benefit of their clientele. From this basis the value of constructing a model of a slide library which could usefully demonstrate a balanced and co-ordinated approach to the management of such a bank of pictorial information can be made clear. Furthermore, the theory of such an idealized library can then be applied to the practical issues and problems met in the day-to-day management of established slide collections.

Working definitions for slide collections

The slide format
The slide is one form of transparency and, therefore, its definition falls within that of the transparency. 'A transparency is a positive, two dimensional monochrome or colour image on a transparent base stock, such as film or glass, viewed by transmitted light.' The slide being a special transparency can be further, more narrowly described. 'A slide is a transparency usually produced by photographic processes, commonly in the 35mm format, rigidly mounted in a 2 × 2 inch frame, and viewed on a screen with the aid of appropriate still projection equipment.'[14] It should be said immediately that although the 35mm size is the format produced in the greatest numbers, and is familiar to most people, mainly because of its continuing popularity with the press and amateur photographers over many years, numerous other sizes of transparency do exist. Table 1 lists the principal sizes.

FORMAT NAME	PICTURE SIZE	OUTSIDE FRAME SIZE	COMMENTS
100 Film (sub miniature)	17 × 12 mm	30 × 30 mm 1.25 × 1.25 inch	Uses standard projection equipment
126 Film (Instamatic)	28 × 28 mm	50 × 50 mm 2 × 2 inch	ditto
35mm (half frame)	24 × 18 mm	50 × 50 mm 2 × 2 inch	ditto
35mm (square frame)	24 × 24 mm	50 × 50 mm 2 × 2 inch	ditto
35mm (full frame)	36 × 24 mm	50 × 50 mm 2 × 2 inch	ditto
127 Film	40 × 40 mm	50 × 50 mm 2 × 2 inch	Now uncommon
220 Film	60 × 4.5 mm	70 × 70 mm 2.75 × 2.75 inch	Special large projection equipment
120 Film	60 × 60 mm 2.25 × 2.25 inch		
–	127 × 102 mm 5 × 4 inch	Larger formats unmounted	This size and larger not normally projected
–	7 × 5 inch		
Half plate	6.5 × 4.75 inch		
Full plate	216 × 165mm		
–	8.5 × 6.5 inch		
–	10 × 8 inch		

Table 1   Transparency and slide sizes

The dominance of 35mm is rooted in its optimum size. While not producing the image quality of the larger formats, the smaller size of 35mm cameras, the range of accessories available, particularly interchangeable lenses, and the ease of handling and portability of the equipment, combine to make 35mm the best compromise for many working photographic situations. The format also has the advantage for the slide manager that a large collection can be compactly stored and this can be a decisive factor when the creation of a collection is being proposed and there are competing claims for office or library floor space.

In theory there is no reason why all that applies to the library management of the 35mm slide size cannot be applied to the other formats. However, the usage of slides both smaller and larger than 35mm differ from the popular format quite considerably. Although it has not been researched, it is unlikely that systematically organized collections of the formats smaller than 35mm exist in any substantial numbers. While the formats larger than 35mm do exist in large numbers and in systematically managed collections, their main use is for quality reproduction in magazines and journals and not for lending for projection or for the purpose of instruction by direct use of the subject matter of the illustrations. The larger formats are, therefore, more closely related in collection management terms to photographic negatives, whereas the 35mm slide is more closely tied in this connection to positive pictures of all types. Table 2 gives the sizes of glass lantern slides.

United Kingdom	82.5 × 82.5 mm	3.25 × 3.25 inch
United States	101.5 × 82.5 mm	4 × 3.25 inch
Europe	85 × 85 mm	3.25 × 3.25 inch
	100 × 85 mm	4 × 3.25 inch

Table 2   Glass lantern slide sizes

Although the glass lantern slide is archaic, valuable collections exist as original historical source material in libraries, archives and private collections. The fragility of glass slides is such that the images need reproducing to ensure their preservation. Not only is the glass brittle, but the delicate and ageing emulsions are vulnerable to moisture and even mildly corrosive agents.

Clearly, it is the modern full-frame 35mm slide which demands attention in slide libraries containing currently relevant and active material and which exist to fulfil the same broad purposes as do other libraries which hold a combination of print and non-book media.

The collection

Collections of slides or collections containing slides can be variously composed of:

1 Slides within tape/slide sequences.
2 Slides in discrete packages in a predetermined order or a set.
3 Individual slides which usually, but not necessarily, relate to other slides in the collection.

When slides are included in a tape/slide sequence they, in effect, become an integral part of another medium of communication. Although the visual information is the dominant feature and message-transmitting element of the tape/slide, the introduction of sound, whether it is a spoken commentary, music or sound effects, fundamentally changes the way in which the pictorial element is received. The visual image as a result becomes part of a predetermined programme and its purpose within the programme closely defined to provide a constituent part of the whole message to be communicated. Fixed links and associations are created with the sound and vision immediately before and after the individual slide and its accompaniment and with the programme as a whole. An illustration is used for one specific purpose within the programme although it may contain a wealth of other uses and connections as an individual image. It follows directly from this that the use of an individual image is not fixed in this way, but is free to be used in innumerable connections. In practice, of course, slide libraries of individual images are usually used flexibly and in differing combinations to cover a wide band of connections within an overall broadly defined subject area.

Slide sets by comparison are also designed like the tape/slide for specific programme objectives and are in that sense nearer to the tape/slide as a medium of communication in the way they are normally employed. Individual slides can of course be extracted from tape/slide sequences or slide sets to fulfil other requirements, but the inconveniences of doing this on any extensive scale in a busy library working situation is likely to be problematic and possibly unworkable.

In a pure sense the true slide library is that which has been referred to by one primary source as made up of 'unitary images'.[15] This distinction is important since, as mentioned above, whereas the tape/slide sequence and the slide set can be successfully integrated in conventional library shelving arrangements the collection of single images by its very nature requires segregated treatment. Clearly, almost any body of slides can be grouped into subsections to form sets in fixed sequences and it is a crucial management decision to choose to do this or to make the basic unit of the collection the single image. This has a fundamental effect on the amount of processing work which is required in identifying, labelling, classifying, cataloguing and indexing. There is no escape from the fact that the collection of unitary images requires considerably more labour to establish, administer and maintain than does a collection of slide sets, but it is also inescapable that such work is an absolute necessity to fulfil the specific needs that such a collection is constructed to meet. Where a variety of users demand that specific images are retrieved for particular purposes and no substitute is adequate, then the unitary slide collection and its attendant work-intensive qualities have to be confronted and undertaken. Attempting to use a slide collection composed of sets to answer queries for specific illustrations is unsatisfactory to the user and unprofessional for the manager. Fortunately for the slide manager the introduction of ever more powerful micro computers in the latter half of the 1980s has made it possible to provide a means of reducing some of the tedious manual work involved in running a slide library. Also, a greater number of approaches to the material can be provided as can fuller descriptive details, customized print-outs for borrowers, for example, and identification labels for slides. Such automation reduces significantly the volume of manual work involved in managing any slide collection and frees personnel for other work. Although it is possible to admix slide sets and single images in the same storage system and sequence, this can be confusing to users.

Although it would be useful to draw a distinction between the terms slide collection and slide library, it is perhaps too early in the professional standardization of slide management to offer formal definitions. However, the term, collection, is self-evidently more general and can be used to denote the accumulation of a body of slides which is not as systematically structured as a slide library, does not possess developed retrieval devices or does not necessarily serve a clearly defined user group. It can be supposed that such parameters do exist or have been established when a body of slides is referred to as a slide library. It is, for example, unlikely that a personal collection of slides, however well developed, could be referred to as a library since access is presumably limited and retrieval devices likely to be designed to meet only the requirements, at least initially, of the individual originator. Under such circumstances the term collection would be more appropriate.

The criticism has been made that slide library is a contradiction in terms, but it is now accepted in most connections that 'library' refers to collections of information materials which include items other than print material alone, although a strong association and assumption persists, particularly in many library users' minds, that the librarian's sole concern is books and conversely that managers of audio-visual materials are not conversant with print-based libraries. The term 'slide bank' has been used by some writers, but without definition or particular clarification being offered. The use of all these terms appears to be mildly affected by the ties or associations a collection has with well-established existing libraries. A collection is more likely to be referred to as a slide library if it is an integral part of a library service in for example a college of art. Where a slide collection exists apart from a print-based library the term slide library is less likely to be used. Such a relationship often exists, and is exemplified, in the medical teaching environment where substantial slide collections are usually located in Departments of Medical Illustration within Teaching Hospitals and not in Medical Libraries.

The question of what size of slide collection constitutes a library is ultimately one of reasonable personal judgement. Clearly, only a few slides can hardly be referred to as a library, a term which implies there are a sufficient number of slides to comprehensively cover a finite subject area, however narrow. One drawer of a standard filing cabinet can hold approximately 3,600 slides in 150 suspended plastic pocket files each holding 24 slides. From this it can be seen that a collection of 1,000 slides is very insubstantial in library terms although of course it can represent a valuable collection if composed of unique images. It is only when a collection exceeds about 4,000 slides that more sophisticated retrieval devices need to be considered. However, when a new slide collection is planned it is likely in many instances that it will grow from nothing to in excess of 4,000 slides in a short space of time. In such circumstances it is sound professional sense to anticipate developments and establish procedures which take into account the management problems associated with an intermediate-sized collection. Broadly, an intermediate-sized slide collection or library will number between 10,000 and 100,000 slides. Although it cannot be substantiated here, there are suggestions that large collections, i.e. in excess of 100,000 slides, encounter problems engendered by the sheer number of slides involved and with existing microcomputer systems. Such collections are also almost certainly to have been begun before modern database management systems were introduced and, therefore, will necessarily have to have a great deal more work carried out on retrospective catalogue conversion to new systems.

The slide manager

A wide range of terms have been and are used to describe the persons managing slide collections. The more common ones in use are:

Audio-visual librarian
Custodian
Media librarian
Picture librarian
Resources librarian
Slide curator
Slide librarian
Slide manager
Slide technician
Visual resources librarian

Many other titles and combinations exist. In many cases appropriate titles are devised by employers or more senior managers, often with a subject prefix, to fit particular job descriptions and are unique to the post held.

Naturally, it is not possible to stipulate which of these terms should or should not be employed, but under present circumstances where a wide variety of working situations are evident where slides collections are maintained, the all-purpose term 'slide manager' appears to be most appropriate. Should the moves, within the sphere of visual arts libraries, towards establishing a clear identity for slide managers emerge then no doubt an acceptable label will be established and welcomed. Activity in this area is centred, as so often, on the Art Libraries Society (ARLIS/UK and Ireland) and through its links with similar affiliated bodies in other countries, in particular ARLIS/NA. Other bodies representing interests in this connection are the Visual Resources Association (VRA), the visual resources committee of the Mid-America College Art Association (MACAA) and the Institute of Medical and Biological Illustration (IMBI).

The fight by visual resource curators for professional recognition in the US is well documented in a special issue of *Visual Resources*.[16] This is essential reading for those similarly placed in the UK. If developments are to be mirrored in the UK, with appropriate adjustments allowing for the different scale of personnel numbers and geography, then the organizational aspects of the VRA's active expansion and development could provide a useful model. All that emanates from the VRA is highly relevant to all working with pictorial material not only to those in the visual arts, but in all other disciplines where images are used and generated.

The purpose of slide collections and the needs of clientele
It is desirable that the aim or purpose for any slide collection is clearly laid out in a formal written statement or at the very least is clear in the minds of those managing the collection. In reality the purpose of the parent organization either dictates or strongly determines the subject scope of the illustrations collected. The comprehensive list of types of slide-holding organization included above (see page 18) indicates immediately the necessary purpose of any slide collection in that organization. However, it does not indicate which user groups within a particular organization are necessarily served. Research suggests that in the medical context, for example, slides are used primarily and extensively for medical teaching or as a record of patients' conditions.[17] Other user groups such as medical students, General Practitioners, paramedical and nursing students have less direct access or are simply not catered for and are, therefore, less well served by the same collections. Clearly, slide collections which have grown up possibly from the initiative and active involvement of one user group, and to serve their needs, can have a potential to fulfil the needs of others and the absence of this is not always immediately apparent. It may be natural to assume that a slide collection in a particular organization serves the needs of all, or a majority of, the personnel within that organization, but this assumption can be misleading with some collections only serving subordinate groups with specialist interests. Since one of the economies afforded by libraries, or any substantial collection of centralized information resources, is the maximizing and constant reuse of stock, it is desirable that all potential user groups are identified and that they are ultimately provided with the service they require. Unless such conscious steps are taken and articulated it is possible for unnecessary

under usage to occur with a consequent waste of funds and for legitimate client needs to go unsatisfied.

Parameters other than or linked to the immediate purpose of the parent organization in which a slide collection is located also apply in determining the scope of a collection. Some of these are listed below.

Subject coverage	Broad or narrow.
Clientele	Private or public.
Extent of catchment	International, national or local.
Funding	Commercial, charity or publicly financed.
Function	Archival, current information, education, entertainment/leisure, or research.

This chapter has ranged over the whole fragmented, disjointed and steadily changing scene of slide management in known collections in a variety of situations. It needs to be emphasized that indications are that there are a large number of collections in the UK whose existence and management methods are still unrecorded and unresearched.

The following chapters concentrate on more particular aspects of slide management and the climate of change due to technological innovation.

2 The literature of slide collection management

The background and development

Although slides are a distinct photographic format familiar to almost everyone, they have, historically, neither been a major category of stock in most libraries nor have they been at the forefront of discussions or developments within AV librarianship or picture librarianship.

Taken in its entirety the professional literature from both librarians and other slide collection managers is testament to the fact that the management of slides has been reported in a fragmentary way and this area of information work has not been brought fully into the mainstream of library literature or acknowledged library practice. Indeed it has to be recognized that an important reason for this is that a substantial degree of activity concerning slide usage and the accumulation of slides in structured collections has taken place and continues to take place outside what would traditionally be regarded as the library profession. In 1982 in the US, the Visual Resources Association (VRA) emerged as a separate professional body to represent the distinct interests of slide curators. This organization brought together all with an interest in picture resources irrespective of their former professional backgrounds or qualifications. The establishment of the VRA and its significance will be discussed shortly. In addition to differences in professional identity there also exists a division of function. This essentially involves the divide between academic-based collections and those of commercial picture supply.

Personnel working in picture agencies, collecting pictures and possibly creating and supplying slides, would not normally identify their work with that of an art library in an academic institution, for example, and are unlikely to have any professional contact or communication with conventional non-commercial library activities. Such staff are also unlikely to see their work and the management of their collections as having a common link or similarity with slide collections maintained in many publicly-funded organizations. A different level of documentary background and descriptive detail of slide stocks appears to be the main discernible difference between collections used for academic study or research and those which exist as reservoirs of pictures for re-publication, where swift location and supply of illustrations is the paramount requirement. Nevertheless, although the clientele, the stock, and even the collections' root purposes may vary considerably, a common denominator does exist on the simple practical basis that pictorial information in slide form is stored and needs to be effectively retrieved for subsequent use. When considering the searchers' needs or the national or international provision of slide resources all slide collections are relevant, whatever the specific narrower aims or reasons for existence of any particular individual collection.

In addition to the fact that there is an apparent lack of theoretical literature covering slides from the commercial picture world, the literature from mainstream librarianship and picture librarianship is also incomplete and fragmented. Since slides are a special format within picture librarianship, which is itself an area not extensively covered by the professional literature, it is perhaps not surprising that slides have gone largely unnoticed by the majority of information professionals who are not immediately concerned with slide management. The value of slide collections has, naturally, always been acknowledged by those working solely or principally with other picture formats in picture libraries. However, in general terms slides have been and remain a neglected area of librarianship and many multidisciplinary and mixed format collections are often undervalued by the organizations and institutions in which they exist and by some general users of resource collections. Where slide collections are maintained alongside more traditional library materials they are sometimes seen as ancillary or arcane.

In times of financial stringency such collections are also taken to be a luxury or an optional extra, expendable and therefore vulnerable to cost-cutting. In some instances resource managers may view the sacrifice of such collections as a means of protecting traditional library stocks of print material or the funds to finance them. Slide collections share this threat to their furtherance or existence with other minor categories of stock and audiovisual collections. This is particularly so when they can be readily and immediately compared with much more substantial core collections of materials, usually books. Such a malaise also affects the creation of collections since many library or resource managers insist on extra funding to initiate new collections and when funding is not forthcoming they are then reluctant to proceed in establishing a collection and new service.

In the UK, at least, indications are that for these and other reasons slide collections may not exist in situations where they would otherwise be appropriate, and where a slide collection could meet a perceived or obvious user need. Also, where small collections do exist, they are underutilized and underdeveloped for similar reasons. Moreover, it is evident that a cycle of indifference towards slide library practices has been evident in the past. A lack of research studies does not stimulate an exchange of information which leads to local practices proliferating without generating further reports in the literature and so on. Where relatively detailed work is carried out it has not been generally followed up or consolidated to provide the professional continuity necessary for recognized standards of practice. Indications are that this state of affairs is drawing to a close and that the diligent work which continues to be carried out principally by ARLIS and the VRA is providing the formulation of standards and new, more authoritative standard publications.[1]

Although this is the universal picture when considering collections in all fields there are, by contrast, initiatives from within special subject fields and there has been greater activity in the US than in other parts of the English-speaking world. One of the most significant advances in the US was the creation in 1982 of the Visual Resources Association (VRA) which has a primary interest in slide collections. In effect this organization has established the recognition of the profession of visual resources curatorship, at least in the US, by including in its membership a wider circle of personnel than qualified librarians who may manage picture collections. Many concerns of the VRA are held in common with the Visual Resources Division of the Art Libraries Society of North America (ARLIS/NA) and the College Art Association (CAA) and there are co-operative ventures involving the three bodies. The VRA has a significant publishing output which is international in scope and outlook rather than confined to the US or North America. It would be difficult to formulate practical definitions of picture librarianship and visual resources curatorship which would provide any useful distinction between the two expressions. Nevertheless the VRA has been instrumental in establishing the ascendancy and recognition of the term visual resources collection in the US.

The term *visual resources collection* has evolved as a description for what was formerly called a photograph and/or slide library or collection. The most likely reasons for this transition are to reflect the increasing variety in visual formats being collected today and to avoid the impression that such a collection provides the same kind of access and service as a book library. A visual resources collection is any organisation or unit having as its primary function the collection of photographic images for such purposes as research, teaching, or historical documentation.[2]

The emergence of the term visual resource collection stems from the fact that in the US, the substantial collections of visuals which exist, clearly isolated from book libraries, have won collective recognition and have established and are increasing their profile. Such developments bring benefits to slide management advancement since they bring together people from within and outside mainstream librarianship who have a common interest. Such relationships have not been developed to the same extent in the UK or elsewhere.

However, it is to be regretted that mainstream librarianship was not flexible or foresighted enough to accommodate and incorporate fully the personnel and the concerns of visual resources management. Such a development would have provided for closer ties between people who have after all the common factor of managing information, be it textual, moving or still visuals, which are growing ever more integrated in their use through the new multimedia technologies. Although it is possible with hindsight to make this judgement, it has to be acknowledged that when the VRA was established, mainstream, traditional, print-based librarianship still had an ambivalent attitude towards audio-visual and pictorial media. Education for librarianship in the US or the UK did not cater fully for these formats and picture librarianship remained something of a marginalized activity. This contributed to and encouraged the establishment of separatist organizations which represented the collective needs and interests of staff engaged in the practical working management of picture collections. On the other hand it is evident that specialist organizations are often particularly dynamic and when international links are established, as in the case of ARLIS, then significant progress can often take place which would be unlikely under the auspices of more generally orientated professional bodies.

However, as far as the literature is concerned, and despite the above, the sum of the parts of the reported activity in slide management in special subject areas does not add up to a whole cohesive body of accepted practice, and falls well short of what could be considered a developed librarianship of slides. While excellent individual slide collections exist in terms of their organization and exploitation, there are few examples of established links, a cross fertilization of ideas or exchange of working practices between subject disciplines, and as a result there are no signs that an agreed or accepted common core of recognized practice is emerging.

The whole evolution of the slide's development as a photographic format and as an item in structured library collections has contributed to the present-day situation and this is again being modified and made more complex by the influence of electronically-generated pictures. The far-reaching implications of new technological developments are set to pervade the whole field of picture libraries in the future and the implications of this are covered in more detail in Chapter 8.

As mentioned earlier, an important contributory reason for the lack of a sizeable overall literature, accepted texts or a more standardized approach to slide collection management is that many slide collections are efficiently managed by personnel outside librarianship in the sense that such people are not formally trained in librarianship or that their collections often have no institutional or organizational connection with a print-based library. This is much more the case in the US than in the UK where often, but by no means always, slide collections have closer connections with conventional library systems. Frequently in the many cases which exist where collections are not linked to libraries the custodians have strong connections with, or are drawn from, the slides' user group, and are specialists in the subject field of the slides held. Alternatively, or in addition they may have technical photographic expertise used in the actual production processes of the slides, and are not trained information professionals. The expertise developed by such slide specialists in all aspects of slide management has in many cases, through no fault on their part, been unavailable to other interested parties. This has been because of individual professional isolation or because separate professional groupings have tended to circulate their methods only within a closed circle of immediate contacts. There is also the further fact that the practical necessities of everyday working life often leave no time for discussion or contributions to journals. In some cases it is probable that individuals working alone in widely differing subject fields may simply consider their everyday working solutions to their own problems unworthy of reporting in any professional journal or consider them of little interest to others outside their special subject concerns. Since their main preoccupation is quite naturally centred on their own subject field or the specialized function of their collections, it is perhaps not the first reaction of such personnel to think in terms of the picture format, as such, with which they are working, rather than the subject matter which it contains. Consideration of the slide as a special picture format for universal subject matter is, at least initially, a theoretical pursuit yet one which ultimately should have a bearing and impact on the practical organization of slide collections particularly large, or multidisciplinary collections.

Within librarianship as a whole, therefore, the literature relating to slide collections has not developed substantially beyond slide managers reporting on their own collections. This is particularly true of the literature in the UK. Historically, from the mid-1960s in the US, it is noteworthy that serious attempts were made to devise universally applicable methods of slide classification and indexing, for example, which demanded a large measure of theoretical understanding for what was being proposed. These events generated some reaction, discussion and exchange of developed opinion on slide management which it appears has not occurred before or since to quite the same extent. However, whereas it could be assumed that time would pass these early developments by, they have endured and re-emerged to be seen as far sighted. This is particularly so of the Santa Cruz scheme of Simons and Tansey which continues to be used, respected and influential in the US if less so elsewhere.[3] Although the scheme of Simons and Tansey anticipated the expansion of automated methods it is still remarkable that it has survived so well the dramatic developments in computing technology, and in particular the application of database packages to slide retrieval.

It would perhaps be natural, but largely mistaken to assume that knowledge of some definitive method of slide management resides within formal librarianship, either explicitly or by a direct application of techniques or methods used to retrieve or manage other library formats, principally of course printed material. However, it can be reasonably assumed that librarianship and the wider professional information community is the most appropriate place for co-ordinating discussion, the exchange of ideas and for movement towards standardizing some working practices. It is rather in the task of collecting, interpreting and possibly unifying the existing practices from a number of subject fields from both library affiliated and non-library associated collections where helpful progress though problematical is possible.

It is not useful or instructive to exhaustively review all the contributions relating to slide collection management in detail. The rapid development of automated methods and their now pressingly relevant application in the future, even for relatively small collections, has made many early reports of much reduced value for today's needs. A sharp upturn is evident in both the number and the renewed enthusiasm of contributions to the periodical literature concerned with image and slide management over approximately the last four years (i.e. 1989–1993). This period can be seen as a distinctively new era characterized by the potential for advancement in 35mm slide library development brought about by the increased data-handling capacities of microcomputers, the introduction of optical disc technologies and the prospect of high definition television.

The existing literature on slide collection management consists mainly of reports on how individual collections are managed and on aspects of retrieval. There are less than a handful of monographs on slides and much of the activity is based in the US.[4] There are few up-to-date research studies which are concerned with an overall view of the field.

Using a chronological approach it is helpful to consider the contributions to slide management literature in three periods of quite widely differing durations.

1   From the earliest mention of slides up to approximately 1983.
2   From around 1983 to 1989.
3   From about 1989 to date.

Although the automated retrieval of slides prior to about 1982 was possible for those with the necessary finances for computing resources and had been developing in theory from the 1960s it was only with the introduction of microchip technology in the early 1980s that it became realistic for medium-sized slide collections to be managed via in-house microcomputers. However, it was not until the late 1980s that both sufficient memory and faster processors became available which could handle the data quantity and information retrieval requirements of sizeable slide banks. Also during the 1980s the development of 'off the shelf' database software packages greatly facilitated slide library management. By about 1989 not only had a good choice of these packages been made commercially available, but also by that date the potential of CD data storage was also beginning to exert a strong influence on picture storage and retrieval.

The period up to approximately 1983

From the earliest times of hand-painted glass slides in the seventeenth century, through the time of the invention of photography in the 1830s, and up to the period preceding the economic boom of the 1960s, the glass lantern slide was produced and used in an increasingly large number of academic institutions. Although 35mm colour slides had been produced and maintained in structured collections since their first appearance in the 1930s it was not until the 1960s that the increase in economic well-being led to a corresponding expansion in funds allocated to education. This in turn brought about an increase in the number and size of slide collections in this important area.

Visual arts institutions, and their associated libraries and personnel figured prominently and almost exclusively in the use and organization of slide collections. In many cases, however, collections were located in faculty departments and not in libraries and were not administered by specialist staff. This is confirmed by the general reviews of the literature relating to slides; by Frietag and Irvine,[5] Irvine,[6] both in the US, and by Bradfield[7] in the UK, though the UK reference refers mainly to more recent times. Frietag and Irvine give some indication of the early interest in slide management by stating that their search of periodical indexing services for the period 1874–1970 yielded only 24 articles. Whereas a functional outline sketch of slide library history confined to the visual arts area is provided for the

US there is no correspondingly convincing account available for the UK.

Almost all early reported information relates to the visual arts subject area and to the academic environment. The development of slide collections in the commercial sphere, in the medical field and all other fields would appear to require much original research. There are indications, however, that interesting source material does exist which would justify further investigation. One quotation from an eminent contributor will perhaps suffice here.

A generation ago the lantern slide was little known except in magic lantern entertainments, and it required some courage for the first schools to make it a part of the educational apparatus. Today there is hardly a college or university subject which is not receiving great aid from the lantern. No one thinks of it as a course in art or discusses it from an ethical standpoint. It is needed by the engineer, physician, botanist, astronomer, statistician, in fact in every conceivable field, but of course, it is specifically adapted to popular study of fine arts because they are so dependent on visual examples, and the lantern is the cheap and ready substitute for costly galleries.[8]

This was written by Melvil Dewey in 1906. The passage is quite startling for the insight it exhibits into the potential of the pro-jected image for visual instruction and in pointing out the value of the lantern slide for instruction purposes across a range of dis-ciplines, particularly by including the applications in science and technology. The quote indicates also a much greater activity outside the visual arts area than is the overall initial impression left by the subsequent literature. It is perhaps important to remember that in earlier times the lantern slide did not have to compete with the rival picture-making technologies which so dominate life today. Clearly, the showing of lantern slides dur-ing this era would be a somewhat more dramatic and com-pelling occasion than is the familiar present day watching of the ubiquitous television. In this sense it can be argued that the slide has moved from near centre stage as a visual format, to a more subsidiary role as a minor visual format, and has been somewhat relegated in the general public's concept of their requirements and expectation of picture information. Against this the widespread use of the slide in professional picture-making circles has, of course, continued to expand. The principal association of the slide in the popular imagination is that of tiresome holiday snaps! However, it is testament to the lasting value of the still picture in the slide format and the quality of the projected picture produced, that the slide endures today in the face of competition from so many other picture formats. Furthermore, it is only with the latest technology that a serious challenge is being posed to the picture resolution provided by the slide and there is still some way to go yet before the electronically-produced television or screen-displayed picture truly equals that of the slide.

Logically it follows without research being necessary that the expansion in 35mm collection development was tied to the technical development of the 35mm slide size, to the coming of colour film in the 1930s and to the fact that by definition collections could not predate the existence of the format! Clearly, with respect to the subject matter of illustrations, material could effectively transcend formats through copying. Although no facts seem to be immediately available it is reasonable to assume that some older illustrative matter was copied to 35mm as soon as the format became available. This could have been to preserve illustrations which were vulnerable on the fragile glass slide format (although black-and-white negatives or prints are a superior archival format to slides), or because the new miniature slide was generally more convenient to handle and project. For a short, but indeterminate period in the 1920s and early 1930s, between the invention of the 35mm still picture camera and the introduction of colour processes, black-and-white 35mm slides were produced in some numbers. Indeed it is recorded that there was some controversy surrounding the introduction of the arbitrary colour standards of the new colour slides. Many art historians preferred to retain black-and-white lantern slides rather than interpret what they considered the inaccurate colour representations provided by the three colour process.

These and other such events and the basic history are well and interestingly covered by Irvine's various contributions to slide library literature.[9] Irvine's principal work, *Slide libraries*, is a monument in the field and provides a central point of reference for almost all other contributions. The photographs and plans of slide libraries and equipment will ensure the work remains of interest as an historical record of slide library practice when its current value has expired. For a brief tracing of the very early history of the hand-painted lantern slide and its projection in the seventeenth century see also Gunther.[10] It is interesting and somewhat surprising that a survey of slide libraries in colleges, universities and museums in the US conducted by Irvine as late as 1968 revealed the fact that over half of the respondents had sufficient glass lantern slides to justify having projection equipment for both the lantern slide and the 35mm format.

It is a feature of contributions to slide library literature throughout all periods that many concentrate on reporting on how individual collections are managed often without reference to practices elsewhere. As Irvine stated over 20 years ago.

What has been especially needed, however, is a philosophy for slide classification and cataloguing, not merely a recitation of the details of a particular system which happens to function adequately for one particular situation.[11]

Irvine also points out how the lack of standardized practice and the great variety of situations in which slide collections are found translates into serious communication problems when attempting a survey by questionnaire.

Because there has never been an attempt to define precisely the various operations and procedures practised in slide collections, it was quite difficult to write a questionnaire that could be understood in exactly the same manner by everyone reading and answering it.[12]

It cannot be claimed that there has been substantial advancement in establishing unifying practices or in creating guidelines in the intervening years. Although it has to be acknowledged that interest was generated in the 1970s in the US when the Mid-America College Art Association (MACAA) provided a focus for interest in slide libraries. Subsequently a number of guides and standards were prepared and published.[13]

Early expressions of co-operation and consultation such as these appeared initially as isolated examples or surges of interest rather than as a sustained level of background commitment. Often initiatives appear to have been centred on a group of highly motivated individuals. With the passing of time their enthusiasm was not necessarily transferred to others and developments lost their momentum. In this way the ideas did not become consolidated or absorbed into accepted practice and individual image collections were obliged to continue with local practices, often working from first principles. The cumulative effect of incremental advances has eventually built and gained momentum in the US, and the VRA is now a vibrant organization providing the much needed broader-based focus which was lacking in earlier years.

During the late 1960s and throughout the 1970s, again in the US, two significant initiatives were forthcoming. Although their importance and applicability has diminished substantially with the passing of the 20 years since their publication, the work of Diamond[14] and of Simons and Tansey[15] were contemporary minor landmarks in the theory and practice of slide retrieval. The chief merit of the two initiatives was their effort to consider the problems of slide retrieval without the prejudice of adapting methods first used with other materials. Both Diamond, and Simons and Tansey recognize the manifold uses of pictorial material and both set out to devise systems which would provide numerous approaches to the pictorial information. Although Simons and Tansey purported to be devising a 'universal classification system', and they include schedules for science and history, the detachment from an overall art history/visual arts bias or involvement is not convincing. A critique of Simons and Tansey's scheme is contained in Wright's contribution to *Picture Librarianship*.[16] Whereas Simons and Tansey propose a limit of 15 fields by which to record different facets of a slide's description, Diamond suggests no limit and favours indexing in depth. Wright does not favour the indexing of uses of pictures in this way, but advocates confining indexes to aspects more directly associated with the illustration. A good review of the various arguments concerning picture indexing is provided by the later contribution of Krause[17], who is in favour of detailed index coverage for pictures. There appears to be no definitive answer to these difficulties. Clearly, the subject scope of a collection, the service required by the users and the cost/staff time factors, effectively dictate or strongly influence the possible indexing levels in working situations and no substitute is likely for sound, local, professional judgement in deciding what level of indexing to adopt.

The foregoing relates to initiatives essentially from the visual arts with tentative efforts in some cases to broaden the application of what had been developed. When considering other subject areas over the same period, only in the medical field could there be said to be any literature which indicated constructive thinking about slide management. The appearance in 1975 of Strohlein's monograph provided the area with a worthy reference point for development work.[18] Now dated and long out of print the work remains interesting reading not only for students of slide management in the medical area, but also for those with a more general interest. Often with a turn of humour Strohlein begins by posing relevant questions, discusses many fundamental points and is forward looking for the time in recommending preparation for the application of computers to solve slide management problems. Strohlein provides what appears to be a uniquely useful review of a number of classification schemes relevant to arranging and indexing medical slides. Unfortunately there was no revision of this work or further substantial contributions to begin to provide a real nucleus of literature. In many ways the literature in this area misrepresents the relatively well-organized and structured basis which exists for medical slides.

Medical illustration is a well recognized and long-established profession and slides play a significant role in recording patient conditions and in providing illustrations for medical teaching and republication. The journal articles of Hedley and Morton[19] and Barker and Harden[20] provide basic management details concentrating on retrieval, and both Tabour[21] and McKenna[22] give accounts of how slide collections have developed by securing the co-operation of a number of individuals with an interest in the systematic organization of slides in the hospital situation.

The period from approximately 1983–89

A small number of contributions to the literature in the early part of this period serve to define its character. Changes and new applications had been developing for a number of years previously, but these had not been formally reported or clarified in the literature.

Delaurier's paper is a landmark contribution, succinctly covering all the essential issues relevant to the management of slides in the visual arts area, as seen at the time, and is an important reference for the student new to the field or requiring a concise overview or introduction.[23] Although the article does not dwell on the retrieval aspects of slide collections Delaurier points out the lack of universally applicable systems.

I think it is safe to say that no two slide collections use exactly and wholly the same cataloguing or classification system.[24]

Delaurier devotes a substantial part of her paper to relating the story of the gradual emergence in the US of professional recognition for those specialists who manage slide collections. Slide curator was the preferred designation at the time, but the term visual resources curator has now become more accepted. Two quotations serve to illustrate the tenor of Delaurier's remarks.

Until a professional is hired, slide collections are usually managed by a professor, a graduate student, a librarian, or by clerical help as an added responsibility.[25]

Although some work with visual media is often included in library science courses, it is generally recognised as inadequate for a position as slide curator without a solid knowledge of art history and experience with slides.[26]

Clearly, at the time of writing the required qualifications specified by Delaurier, namely a master's degree in art history and experience of working with slides, were not being fully provided for by the professional library education programmes. Since this was written in 1982 it is somewhat surprising, for by that time audio-visual librarianship was well established and recognized. Perhaps it is more the subject knowledge in the art history field which was lacking rather than information-handling skills. However, it appears that appropriate education and training in the US in picture librarianship was not available at the necessary level within the existing educational framework for library science graduates. Delaurier notes the significance of the few specially developed and designed courses for slide curators which aided greatly the ultimate establishment of a specialist professional identity.

In the first statement above the way in which librarian is implied as being almost as inappropriate to slide management as the other categories of personnel referred to may seem questionable to the present day UK reader. Even before this time, in the UK, and in the intervening time, formats other than the book and print-based material had increasingly asserted themselves as items demanding the attention of the library profession. Latterly a conscious shift in library education has been made away from the concept of the librarian being a book manager towards being an information manager. This has been reflected strongly in the content of degree courses offered and has extended to the renaming of university departments to emphasize information management rather than traditional librarianship. It can no longer be in doubt that pictorial information in all its forms is firmly within the ambit of modern librarianship or professional information work and that the continuing integration of text and illustrations, in image databases for example, is likely to confirm and consolidate this. It was not until the late 1980s though, that this trend reached an openly and fully acknowledged conclusion.

However, since groupings of human individuals are rarely formed on such strictly logical lines, parallel and overlapping developments and interests are almost certain to come about. Unfortunately, as Delaurier goes on to explain, the fact that slide curators belonged to no recognized profession, their status and salaries were determined on a local basis resulting in generally low renumeration even though individuals were effectively dually qualified in terms of subject knowledge and information

skills and in some cases were required to have additional knowledge of languages. Recognition of the status of slide curators in
the US came through support from the College Art Association
(CAA), which is a representative body of art historians, teachers
and academics, and through the Art Libraries Society
(ARLIS/NA). Although many slide curators held membership
of these bodies it was not until the establishment of the Visual
Resources Association (VRA) in 1982 that the distinct professional identity of visual resource curators was given a focal
point. By comparison, the situation in the UK is that although
individuals working with slides seem to be similarly placed it
would appear that they do not exist in sufficient numbers to
bring about the cohesion to achieve or sustain separate recognition. No substantial change has been made since meetings were
held to discuss the status of slide librarians in the mid-1980s.
Davis outlines the UK position at that time.[27]

Delaurier's article provides some useful details of chronology
relating to the founding of relevant bodies in the US.

1969 Slide curators first national meeting within the compass
      of the CAA.
1972 Mid-America College Art Association (MACAA) regional
      group provides umbrella for active visual resources inter-
      ests.
1974 ARLIS/NA begin visual resources group.
1977 Canadian visual resources group formed, meeting
      annually with the Universities Art Association of Canada.
1977 Formal recognition of slide curators by CAA and
      ARLIS/NA.
1978 Initiation of South-East America College Art Association
      (SEACAA).
1982 Foundation of Visual Resources Association (VRA).

For a more wide ranging chronology of developments spanning
the years 1846–1989 see the more recent contribution by Hoort.[28]

Delaurier's paper relates essentially to the visual arts.
Although museums are mentioned there is no elaboration. The
extent and significance of slide collections in museums in the US

or other countries is not well covered, but their existence is not in doubt and they are naturally closely allied to the academic art environment and art galleries and are unlikely to differ significantly from art history slide collections as far as the necessary management techniques are concerned.

Delaurier concludes by providing details of the extensive and developing publications which have emanated from the above groupings and their publishing programmes. In the following decade since Delaurier's paper, many of these publications have become recognized, established and authoritative sources. The international scope of the VRA and the close affiliation of the national representative bodies of ARLIS have made these organizations particularly strong and significant in co-ordinating work in their respective fields in the English-speaking world.

One other reference from this period is of particular significance, but rather as a portend of things to come rather than for its instructional value for present day practice. The contribution of Gilson and Collins is strongly persuasive of the need for the retrieval of slides in structured collections to be automated.[29] The benefits of doing so in principle are clearly made out, even though the storage capacity of the microcomputer used is small compared with present day standards. Another important aspect of the paper is its demonstration of how a large existing collection which has previously been managed manually can be made much more accessible and efficient without extensive physical reorganization through the use of the microcomputer. The paper in effect provides a beginner's guide to how a database can provide so many more approaches to the subject material than can manual methods.

By 1984 the widespread use of microcomputers to manage slide collections were such that broader reviews of applications began to appear. Useful in this connection is Markey's review which provides an overview, mainly from the US perspective and as is almost always the case, from the visual arts subject field.[30]

Towards the end of the time period under consideration the automation of slide collections began to reach a level of development which enabled the data from sizeable libraries to be stored and manipulated without undue regard to limitations of size of microcomputer storage or internal processor speed. The two reports on the development of the automated system LANSLIDE devised at the University of Lancaster to manage the library's visual arts slide collection are essential reading for those who wish to appreciate the advantages that automation offers.[31] The work at Lancaster also serves to illustrate the clearly-defined direction the new technology is taking slide manage-ment, whether or not all managers decide to apply the automated techniques available. Of the two articles, that which appears in *Program* is the more technically orientated. It is testa-ment to the system that it has successfully been made available as a commercial package and has continued to be further devel-oped in the light of user response, their criticisms and develop-ing requirements. Although competition has grown fiercer and the market become more crowded with software packages rele-vant to slide library management, LANSLIDE still appears to be the only stand-alone and self-contained package written by librarians and having as its source or base an academic, working slide collection, at least as far as the UK is concerned.

The period from 1989 to date

Although the periods into which this review of the literature of slide management is divided are somewhat arbitrary, it is a char-acteristic of recent years that reports of computer methods applied to slide management have become more prominent in the literature and led to a resurgence of interest in slide collec-tions for this very reason. The fall in the unit costs of computing combined with the increasing speed and data storage capacities of computer applications has led to extensive developments in both automated retrieval and more general slide management systems, and also of the alternative electronic image-making technologies. Another significant development is the realization of mature publishing programmes by the Visual Resources Association, the Art Libraries Societies, the British Association of Picture Libraries and Agencies and other organizations such as the Museums Documentation Association which now collec-tively offer a range of publications covering the visual resources/slide management field in a more complete way.

Current sources
Highly significant publications by the VRA are Schuller's thorough *Management for visual resources collections* (2nd edn, 1989) and the now well-established *Slide buyers' guide* (6th edn, 1990) currently edited by Norine Cashman. More recent publications include Christine Sundt's *Conservation practices for slide and photograph collections* and a number of professional reference works – *British artists authority list,* from the Yale centre for British art photograph archive edited by Anne-Marie Logan; *Standard abbreviations for image descriptions for use in fine arts visual resources collections,* by Nancy Schuller and *Selected topics in cataloguing Asian art* by Eleanor Mannikka.

The VRA's two quarterly serial publications are the *VRA Bulletin* and *Visual Resources: an international journal of documentation.* The Bulletin in fact dates from before the formal beginning of the VRA when curators formed groupings with the support of the College Art Association (CAA). The Bulletin's former names were successively, the *Slides and Photographs Newsletter* and the *International Bulletin for Photographic Documentation of the Visual Arts.* While the *VRA Bulletin* continues to fulfil a newsletter function, providing up-to-date reports from many slide libraries it also includes 'A running update to Cashman's *Slide buyer's guide'.* This is an invaluable current-awareness source of information for slide acquisition in the visual arts and is international in scope as is much of the VRA's work. The Bulletin includes such topics as advances and applications of electronic imaging techniques and use of 'Dataease' (the commercially available database management system) in slide libraries for retrieval purposes and in conjunction with bar code labels to improve circulation methods. Such concerns and discussions would undoubtedly be of interest to those working with slides in fields other than the visual arts, but regrettably it is doubtful if these contributions and news items reach those managing scientific or technical slide collections or those in the commercial picture or slide library sphere.

Deeper full-length journal articles are reserved for *Visual Resources.* This journal ran initially from 1980–83 under the control of the VRA and latterly from 1986 to date under its present publisher Gordon and Breach, with the VRA retaining editorial control. Unfortunately, the initial cost, the possibility of unfavourable exchange rates and the US slant can lead many UK general academic libraries not to include this journal among their acquisitions. Clearly, the journal is essential to the stock of libraries devoted to, or with a strong interest in, the visual arts and/or pictorial information.

Other bodies producing publications of vital interest are ARLIS/UK & Ireland with *Art libraries journal* and *ARLIS/UK and Ireland news-sheet* and ARLIS/NA with *Art Documentation*. The 'Audio-visual news' section of the News-sheet is particularly noteworthy and a useful co-ordinator of information on new slide sources not to be found elsewhere. In the medical field the *Journal of Audiovisual Media in Medicine* and in the commercial picture library sector *BAPLA journal* are also essential current sources in their respective fields. More generally based, but none the less important for supplying news of current developments is the *Audiovisual librarian: the multimedia information journal* published by the audio-visual groups of Aslib and the Library Association. A number of other journals provide information on slides and fulfil an overlapping function between librarianship, other relevant areas such as computer applications or business subject interests. These include titles such as *Computers in the History of Art (CHART)*, *Program* and *Audiovisual*.

Occasional publications continue to be produced which include slides within their scope. Prime examples are *Guidelines for art and design libraries: stock, planning, staffing and autonomy* and *Art and design documentation in the United Kingdom & Ireland: a directory of resources* (Varley, 1993) both published by ARLIS/UK & Ireland. The fact that up-to-date directories which include details of slide collections are now beginning to appear, is fundamental to encouraging further research work by providing basic quantitative data on the size, range and subject scope of collections. Until recently serious doubts existed concerning even the very existence of collections in some fields. It can only be hoped that funding continues to be made available in the UK to expand and consolidate the initial groundwork already carried out. In this respect the *National directory of slide collections*

(McKeown, 1990) is the widest in scope, essentially and effectively covering the non-commercial sector with the annual *BAPLA directory* (British Association of Picture Libraries and Agencies) covering the commercial collections in membership of the Association.

Of lesser value, but still useful is the British Universities Film and Video Council's (BUFVC) *Distributors: the guide to video and film sources for education and training* (Grant, 1990) which includes some slide collection sources and is an aid to selection as well as supplying location information. In the medical field information on the existence of some slide collections can be deduced indirectly from the membership list of the Institute of Medical and Biological Illustration (IMBI) and the *Directory of medical and health care libraries in the United Kingdom and Republic of Ireland* (Wright, 1992) compiled by the Health and Welfare group of the Library Association. Unfortunately access to the IMBI list can be limited since it is unpublished and only circulated to members of the Institute. The directory referred to confirms the slide holdings of medical libraries, but there is no good, clear and comprehensive directory of slide collections in departments of medical illustration or other hospital departments.

Automated retrieval

The arrival of cost-effective microcomputer systems, networks and software for intermediate-sized libraries has naturally led to more slide collections planning and implementing automation, and this is reflected in the recent literature. A prominent contribution to the literature in this area is that by Waterman.[32] The article is particularly strong on analysing the necessary steps prior to obtaining a system. A thorough, conscious awareness of all existing manual processes is recommended in order to gain all the advantages of automating. All the major necessary considerations are covered including circulation, standardization of terms, subject access and co-operative schemes. A useful list of references and a bibliography relating to the planning of automation is appended.

A more specialized review is that of Collins[33] which details the application of the Omnis III+ database system, using an Apple

Macintosh machine, to the George Washington University Art Department Slide Library of over 100,000 slides. Collins's out- look and advice accords with that of Waterman.

Automation so drastically affects the management of information that questions concerning holdings in the collection which would have taken days or weeks to seek out manually can now be answered in a matter of minutes. Therefore, it is best to consider all possibilities dur- ing the initial planning stages.[34]

and

As the project evolves, it is important to consider each aspect of the data base carefully early on, as it affects the way in which the collection will develop in the future.[35]

There is no doubt that automation brings a new urgency and dis- cipline to collating cataloguing data and in standardizing the forms of the data and indexing practice. It is recommended by Waterman that manual procedures are not simply transferred to a computer, but that the structure and purpose of the systems are examined almost from first principles. In this way the maximum benefit of automation can be realized for what is undoubtedly greater initial staff input at the conversion stage. On this basis it is only prudent to consider such matters as slide label printing, circulation systems (possibly using bar codes), and the printing of customized slide lists for users, as complementary features of an integrated automated slide system. Although strong interest has been centred on the process of automation itself other associ- ated areas have come to the fore and received discussion as a result of the implications of automation.

In the visual arts area assessments have been made of *Art and architecture thesaurus (AAT)* and *Iconclass* and of the viability and desirability of down-loading cataloguing records of slides from co-operative and shared cataloguing projects and Machine Readable Cataloguing (MARC) records. Positive views are expressed by both Pearman[36] and Snow.[37] Pearman points out the western European bias of *AAT* and *Iconclass* and discusses the need to cater for 'object level' cataloguing. In essence this refers to the difference between cataloguing a book which is the 'object' or original in hand and cataloguing a picture or slide which is a 'representation' and not the 'object' or original in hand.

These considerations lead on to the subject structure of art history and the visual arts and how art historians conduct their research and view the significance of their work and the visual and documentary collections they accumulate.[38] Whereas the bibliographic librarian catalogues the summary or topical subject of a book, the slide librarian or visual resources curator can be involved in cataloguing both the topical subject and the iconographical subject-matter of an illustration.

Iconography is, however, a highly-developed academic discipline and method within the larger field of art history studies. It can be defined as the study of symbols used in particular styles of visual art and their meaning, but extends beyond description and systematic grouping of subjects, themes and motifs to the direct and implicit meanings of representations. As iconography has developed, the interpretative, conceptual and allegorical aspects of the study have increasingly been referred to as iconology.[39] For the student who wishes to pursue this complex area the work of Markey discusses the automated retrieval of visual resources and provides a good summary of the theory of iconographical classification and method for analysing the subject-matter and meaning in the visual arts.[40] Markey explains the seminal work of Panofsky[41] in formulating the study of visual subject-matter or meaning into three levels – pre-iconographical description, iconographical analysis and iconological interpretation.

This can be an intimidating study for the uninitiated newcomer, but sound indexing of subject-matter can ultimately only be achieved from a thorough understanding of the subject basis and interrelationships of the field to be indexed. Such theory as is embodied in iconographical studies provides this understanding. *Iconclass*, for example, has grown directly from this base over many years in print form and is now also available as a database running under 'Windows' as *Iconclass Browser*.

In a valuable contribution in this connection, Barnett highlights some of the difficulties and clarifies a number of issues.

A few years ago, in a room full of art librarians, when **we** talked about **subjects** we all thought we knew what we were talking about. But today, when **we**, in the broader context of all of us involved in **art documentation** – art librarians, visual resource curators, subject indexers and information managers – use the term **subject** we bring to it many different slants and concepts. Bibliographic librarians tend to define **subject** primarily, though not exclusively, as topical subject following the parameters set by the Library of Congress Subject Headings. Whereas visual resource and object curators and cataloguers tend to define **subject** primarily as the iconographic subject of artwork.[42]

Any system or contribution which eliminates such fundamental confusion is welcome and necessary, but if there are such basic misunderstandings among specialists this naturally compounds the problems for students or practitioners new to the field. A simplified list of the differing levels of subject analysis which have been developed for the visual arts is as follows.

Objective information
Attribution, e.g., creator (artist or photographer)
Title of work
Date created/taken
Physical format
Physical dimensions

Provenance details; details of an item's origins or previous ownership

Topical subjects   e.g.:
Periods of Art History
Techniques
Forms

As used in:
Bibliographic cataloguing
Library of Congress Subject Headings
Art Index
Art and Architecture Thesaurus

Iconographical subjects
Pre-iconographical description; primary subject-matter
Objects depicted, expressional aspects of people or objects, actions being carried out.

Iconographical analysis; secondary subject-matter (as used in *Iconclass*)
Themes, motifs, e.g. story of Samson and Delilah

Iconological interpretation; meaning, significance of symbols

This is a rudimentary list for the purposes of introduction.

It is likely that many intermediate-sized, working slide collections will not require the deeper levels of subject retrieval techniques mentioned here, but awareness of the work in iconography enables conscious decisions to be made concerning the level of subject detail to incorporate in a system.

Furthermore, it is needful to note that *AAT* is a hierarchically arranged list of topical subject terms and that *Iconclass* is an enumerative notational classification scheme of secondary subject-matter and they both share the respective advantages and drawbacks of other subject heading lists and classifications discussed in Chapter 5 (see pages 91–96).

In an original article Small[43] rejects both *AAT* and *Iconclass*, preferring extensive verbal descriptions, many database fields and free text and Boolean searches to effect retrieval. Further discussion of these and related issues are to be found in the writings of Roddy,[44] Roberts[45] and Couprie.[46] Some of the literature makes judgemental comparisons between *AAT* and *Iconclass*, but since they are differently designed retrieval tools operating at differing subject levels, such close criticisms do not compare like with like and are unlikely to lead to balanced conclusions.

Other prominent manual picture/slide cataloguing systems of note and interest to the student are: the Fogg Art Museum, Photograph and Slide Library system, of Harvard University and the Photograph and Slide system of the Metropolitan Museum of Art, New York City.

This concludes the survey of the literature concerned with the management of slide collections as such, but there is a rapidly developing literature based on rival picture-making technologies which purport to offer substitutes for existing banks of picture resources or for which slides are one form of picture input and output.

Although electronic picture-making methods are providing competitive alternatives or have been complementary to the slide, it is the introduction of what has come to be termed 'multimedia' that has created a new need to reassess the place of slide collections in providing banks of illustrations. The emerging sense in which the term multimedia is understood is a simultaneous, sequential or interactive combination of recorded text, sound, still and moving visual media, graphics and animation usually under the control of or generated by a computer. The development of multimedia has been centred on and been made possible by the increasing storage capacity of the optical disc. It is beyond the scope of this review to cover the vast literature covering the technical developments relevant to electronic picture creation. The student should be aware, however, that the near monopoly which conventional photographic production enjoyed has gone forever.

One area of new technology which is more closely related to slide collections and picture libraries is that of image databases. Even the latest journal article is almost out of date before it can be read and one wonders how long it will be before the new technologies themselves are employed to carry instant reports of innovations as they happen! The *Annual review of information science and technology* provides a sober assessment of yearly developments which eliminates some of the sensational, newsy overstatement of some popular press and periodical articles. Contributions are comprehensive and comparative and create an accurate sense of the direction and capabilities of, for example, optical discs.[47] Other contributions which introduce image databases are those of Danziger[48] which convincingly extols the virtues of analogue video disc as a medium for picture storage, and Morton[49] which lucidly compares a number of the analogue and digital storage systems available. Other basic introductory technical details are supplied by Rowland and

Seely.[50] Although knowledge of concepts and general principles can be gained from such articles, it is only fair to point out that any software referred to is likely to have developed considerably since the time of writing.

Some of the main constraints on the successful development of image databases are:

1   Resolution
    Does the resolution compete with the definition possible from conventional photography?

2   Storage capacity
    What is the capacity of the system's storage?
    Does the process of compression and decompression compromise the integrity of the images *vis-à-vis* the purpose of the image collection?

3   Image capture
    Is the process of transferring images from hard copy to the image database convenient, efficient and cost-effective?

4   Can hardcopy images be generated from the database on demand?

5   Can the system cope with foreseeable expansion?

6   Does the retrieval software meet the collection's requirements?

As with all such innovation the forces attributable to the pace of competitive research and development and the successful identification and exploitation of markets, effectively determine what emerges for the end user. Innovation which is successful on the domestic market progressively reduces unit costs and encourages further take-up of the product. Prime examples of this are video recorders and audio CDs. Examples of the opposite are filmless cameras which although they are capable of superb quality images have not made inroads into the amateur conventional photography market. Consequently costs remain high and an impasse is effectively reached where a quality product does not find widespread adoption.

Perhaps the final arbiter of image quality is human perception rather than resolution expressed in the absolute technical terms of pixels or scanning lines. In a thorough article Ester states :

Perceived quality, in the context of image delivery, is a question of users' satisfaction within specific applications. Do images convey the information that users expect to see? What will they tolerate to achieve access to images? Perceived quality is situation dependent: an image level considered acceptable for recognizing a work of art may be objectionable for other purposes. There is also a strong element of efficiency in evaluating delivery-quality images – a good image is one that conveys a maximum perception of quality for the amount of stored data.[51]

Current centres of activity concerning image databases are widespread, but significant report literature emanates from the *International meetings on museums and art galleries image databases*,[52] the Electronics sub-committee of BAPLA and the UK Online User Group (UKOLUG) of the Institute of Information Scientists.

3 Slide acquisitions

Background problems of the materiographic control of slides and their acquisition

Slides can be acquired principally either by purchase or in-house creation. Although donations or the free deposit of slides in collections is not unknown, it is not a planned method of acquisition or one for which the slide librarian is likely to have a strategy. Similarly, where managers have a common interest, arrangements can be established to exchange stock items to the mutual benefit of the participants. Such practices, however, are usually small-scale, local or private agreements and are unlikely to be major sources of new material in general. This is not to denigrate the quality of slides acquired by these methods or to decry the resourcefulness of slide managers in using imaginative ways of improving the range of their collections, and such enterprising methods are always to be commended. Indeed these practices can form a highly desirable component in slide acquisition procedures where formal methods do not provide a full or adequate means to fully develop a collection.

In contrast to the majority of slide libraries, the bulk of traditional print-based library materials in mainstream librarianship have almost always been obtained by purchase. This is to be expected since libraries are inherently collections of information items drawn from the publishing and wider social world in which they exist. Although this may appear to be a superficial statement, slide collections have quite frequently, but not always, had their origin in a specific parent institution with one or more specialized areas of subject interest. The only source of slide input in such instances tends to be found not in the wider world, but in the parent institution itself. This necessarily inward-looking character of slide acquisition has in these cases created uniquely valuable, specialized collections which because of their narrow and unique source of supply are irreplaceable. The main exception to this is visual arts slide libraries who acquire slides from a wide variety of origins, not least of which is purchase from commercial sources, both slide marketing companies and other galleries and libraries.

The bibliographic control of printed media includes systematic cataloguing, listing, and indexing to provide access to the material, as well as evaluative, current and retrospective information on what print items are available. The underpinning basis for this is the law of legal deposit and the concomitant initial recording of publications, on first publication, in the *British national bibliography (BNB)*. This wealth of reliable information coupled with that produced by the commercial publishing world and the book trade, for example in such publications as *Whitaker's books in print*, is so well established that it can be taken for granted that almost any print item can be identified and its source, if extant, located. Similar national bibliographies exist in other countries of the developed world and the net effect of this is that international coverage is good if not exhaustive.

In sharp contradistinction to this, such developed bibliographic service is a luxury unheard of in relation to audio-visual materials. Slides are particularly poorly served even in comparison with other audio-visual formats. Some audio-visual formats, for example video, have a growing number of commercial listings of materiographic details, but lack a central clearing house or any centralized policy of administration. The *British national film and video catalogue* which was such a valuable and successful service for almost thirty years ceased publication in 1992. It would be almost inconceivable for a comparable publication covering items in the print world to disappear quite so abruptly in the same way. The effect of such an event is to throw the searcher back on more original source listings such as publishers' catalogues, publicity and advertising notices and reviews. The librarian or prospective purchaser of such materials has, therefore, to consult many sources as opposed to one or two comprehensive, authoritative sources. The sequential searching of suppliers' catalogues is an inadequate, tedious and unsatisfying method of finding relevant material. Not only can the searcher be faced with the commercial bias of the suppliers' publicity, but also it is often the case that such publications lack indexes detailed or diverse enough to cater for accurate or critical subject enquiries, for example. The piecemeal coverage often leaves the searcher with the feeling that the most relevant item for the purpose either exists and is unlisted, or almost certainly appears in a list which has not come to hand or is difficult to obtain. Furthermore, there can be a lack of objective, evaluative information in some publicity material.

All the foregoing shortcomings apply in their extreme to published or commercially available slide material. Slides emanate from a such a wide variety of sources – from profit- and non-profit-making bodies, companies, academic institutions, leisure organizations, charities and individuals that it is difficult to envisage a workable centralized clearing house which could undertake the work of recording the appearance or existence of such material. Furthermore, it is true to say that no publishing structure exists for slides in the same developed way in which it does for books. Although many specialist slide suppliers/distributors exist, they do not control outlets or dominate the industry as do book publishers. Often slide creators of all types market their slides directly to customers in ways varying from professionally packaged and presented methods to an informal response to enquiries on an *ad hoc* basis.

Nevertheless, an experimental attempt to provide a national listing of audio-visual materials, including slides, did take place between 1979 and 1983 with the issue of the *British catalogue of audiovisual materials (BCAVM)*. This catalogue was a valiant attempt to indicate how the same type of initial recording service could be provided for audio-visual materials as already existed for books. The format adopted was that of *BNB*, with comprehensive entry details according to the Anglo-American cataloguing rules (AACR2) accompanied by complete indexes. Unfortunately, the experimental nature of the publication made it necessary to limit the scope. Entries were based on the materials held by the British Library/Inner London Education Authority Learning Materials Recording Study and excluded video and music. The inclusion solely of educational learning materials, while salutary and laudable, was limiting. In no sense, therefore, could the publication be said to be truly national in coverage or comprehensive in its inclusion of audio-visual formats.

The catalogue remains accessible as an online database (AVMARC), and some further items were added in 1989 although no further supplements of the printed catalogue have been issued. Slides were included in the BCAVM both in the form of sequential sets and as integral parts of tape/slide programmes and thus the work provided a useful source for slide selection at the time. The value of the catalogue has naturally diminished and today it can be considered only as an example of what could be achieved given the investment in money and will. Moreover, as has been indicated earlier, the concern of developed slide libraries is principally for *individual images* and this presents materiographic control difficulties of a different order. These are over and above that which is experienced with packaged audio-visual materials (AVM) as was addressed by the BCAVM with the inclusion of slide sets and tape/slide sequences.

The barriers to progress in the bibliographic control of AVM, including slides, remain.

1 Absence of a legal deposit requirement whereby published AVM pass through a single, national, central control point for recording purposes.

2 The difficulties of enforcing a legal deposit arrangement for AVM should it become law.

3 The fact that many quality avm are not published in the accepted sense or are not commercially available as is the case in the book trade.

4 The fact that the printed word remains culturally if not actually dominant as the perceived medium for information exchange and AVM are perceived as peripheral.

5 This means there is neither the will nor the financial resources available to implement the introduction of legal deposit arrangements or a systematic bibliographic control of avm without legal deposit.

Clearly, these difficulties are compounded when slides, and especially individual slides, are considered. Whereas it is conceivable that some degree of comprehensive centralized recording of the details of discreet published items such as CD-ROMs or video cassettes could be made to function, it is not practical or realistic to expect individual slides or printed pictures to be controlled in a similar manner. As previously indicated the sources are too great in number and the life of many slides can be too short to justify recording their characteristic details. The fragile and often ephemeral nature of the slide is true both in physical terms and on occasions with regard to subject content. For example, slides can be created for one publicity or sales event in the commercial world and afterwards be regarded as expendable.

In view of this, a more likely, effective and fruitful course, in subject specific areas where slides are to be retained for indeterminate periods, is perhaps to adopt a discriminatory approach, selecting the best images for specific purposes or a range of representative images from those which abound. A prime example of such an approach is the *UK national medical slide bank on videodisc*, compiled by Graves Educational Resources and published jointly by Chadwyck-Healey and Graves.

In co-operation with the departments of medical illustration of hospitals throughout the UK a collection of the best medical slides was assembled. From the master collection not only can duplicate slides be bought, but the entire collection is available on videodisc for those who wish to acquire a definitive set of images. It would be wrong to pretend that such a progressive development could be easily repeated in all other subject or academic disciplines, but it is an indication of how new technology can be employed to reduce the difficulties of control posed by a ubiquitous medium such as the slide. Clearly, in the UK at least, slides are a scattered national resource of which few custodians and clientele are fully aware. In many cases individuals are in the process of compiling collections of similar content in various fields and it is likely that benefits will flow from individuals both being aware of other similar collections and also having indirect access to them, for example through the medium of the videodisc.

The pursuit, therefore, of materiographic control for individual slides to emulate or even approach the system which exists for books is always likely to be an unattainable ideal. What perhaps is achievable is the establishment of quality image banks from which definitive images can be obtained in the format as required. This could be either an electronic or conventional photographic format of print or slide. For the prospective development of this approach see McKeown's article on the establishment of a national Centre for Image Information (CII).[1] By such methods the often supposed requirement of comprehensive materiographic control would be shown not to be necessary. It must not go unrecorded that copyright restrictions and respect for the creative rights of artists, photographers and other originators must be incorporated in any developments in exchanging pictorial information on an equitable basis.

Theoretical research and practical work continues into the creation of quality image databases which are likely to have far-reaching effects on how new and existing images are created, stored, viewed and used in the future. Since such databases are designed to carry text to accompany images and provide speedy access through keyword and other indexes, they are destined to become the principal sources for access to illustrations. Their potential to provide materiographic control of images is also profound and it is not rash to predict their use as locating and selection aids for the picture librarian of the future. Until such developments are realized, however, the slide manager is compelled to wrestle with a variety of printed sources which provide incomplete and piecemeal coverage.[2]

Sources for finding slides

Sources of information covering the availability of slides vary from detailed listings by vendors, be they creators, suppliers or distributors providing direct information, to merely indicative sources such as journals or directories which may not be principally concerned with slides or indeed other audio-visual formats. This latter group may require some instinct or intuition on the part of the searcher who, for example, may only be given details of an organization which is judged to possibly provide the slides needed. Under such circumstances only a further enquiry addressed directly to the source can prove conclusive. Also, the enquirer for single slides is frequently required to infer from the information provided whether the required image is contained within a listed packaged set of slides, since it is often the case that slides are marketed only in this form. The necessity for patience in searching under such circumstances is a desirable prerequisite for the librarian building a quality slide collection. One of the main restrictions is that of cost effectiveness. When pursuing a search for a single image perhaps, it may not be worthwhile to conduct a lengthy search if other areas of management work are more pressing. Such judgements are naturally for the individual manager alone to make, for there can be no adequate substitute for practical experience under such conditions.

The sources for slides can, usefully, be broadly categorized for convenience into five groups: (1) US national listings; (2) directories, guides and major suppliers; (3) periodicals; (4) relevant corporate, academic or professional bodies and (5) the catalogues of large prominent individual slide suppliers. Electronic databases either on-line or increasingly on CD-ROM are also available as alternative sources within these categories. As the cost of paper-based production for such services steadily rises and that of on-screen methods of access falls there is likely to come a time when the paper versions will ultimately disappear. The only hard copy would then be the computer print-out produced as a result of specific searches by individuals.

US national listings

Developments in the materiographic control of audio-visual materials in the United States, though not totally comprehensive in coverage, are more substantial than the state of development of such publications in other countries including western Europe and the UK.

The Library of Congress is foremost in co-ordinating activity in addition to holding collections in all formats which are not only of national importance, but of world significance. The general advancement of the educational infrastructure in the US, the wide variety of specialist interest bodies and the overall economic prosperity and magnitude of national resources have all been contributory factors in establishing and developing bibliographical services.

Slide sets, however, have only been included in the catalogues of the Library of Congress since 1972. The relevant section of the *National union catalog* which contains AVM has been variously subtitled over the years as follows.

1953–62   *National union catalog. Motion pictures and*
1968–72   *filmstrips*
1973–78   *National union catalog. Films and other materials for projection*
1983–   *National union catalog. Audiovisual materials*

This latter title appears now on microfiche. Items included are broadly confined to those which have educational and instructional value. It is assumed that the major type of materials excluded are those designed for recreational or entertainment purposes. Although the Library of Congress is the pre-eminent national library body in the US, a number of other organizations are of national, and to varying degrees international, importance.

The National Audiovisual Centre which forms part of the vast administrative structure and resources of the US National Archives and Records Service produces *A reference list of audiovisual materials produced by the US government*. Appearing initially in 1978 the publication is updated by irregular supplements and includes details of slide sets.

Returning to the educational field, the National Information Centre for Educational Media (NICEM) of the University of Southern California formerly issued the *Index to educational slides* which was strongly centred on the visual arts. The service became a database in the shape of AV-ONLINE, accessible through the host DIALOG and is now available as a CD-ROM from Silverplatter Information Inc. Of less direct value to the slide searcher, but of too overall importance to omit is the Educational Resources Information Centre (ERIC). This service, administered under the US Department of Education, provides a wealth of bibliographic information on reports, periodical articles and projects in the educational field. Though slide packages or sources are not listed as such, a judicious use of the references can indicate new sources of images to the moderately experienced user. Whereas the traditional multi-volume printed version of the service made this a somewhat laborious process, the introduction of a CD-ROM version has improved the ease of access and search processes in recent years.

A service from the private sector (though non-profit making) is provided by the Educational Products Information Exchange Institute (EPIE). Much of the emphasis is on the testing and evaluation of educational technology equipment, but a directory of software is produced, entitled *The Educational Software Selector* (TESS).

In the specialized field of medicine the National Library of Medicine (NLM) publishes *The National Library of Medicine audiovisuals catalog* which appears quarterly with annual cumulations

in parallel with the mainstream service of *Index Medicus*, also
from NLM. The corresponding on-line versions are AVLINE and
MEDLINE and the CD-ROM versions are also increasing both in
availability and popularity.

Directories, guides and major suppliers

This section progresses from the more general publications covering wide areas which are appropriate to the process of ultimately locating slides, to those few which concentrate in
particular on the slide as a format. The subject scope ranges from
multidisciplinary to the specialized.

The yearly volume of the *Annual review of information science
and technology* provides an overview of developments in LIS and
is a useful source for checking on trends which are taking place
in image libraries on the occasions when significant events are
reported. Clearly, a number of years may lapse between contributions concerning picture collections being included, but the
concise and authoritative information provided can be a valuable summary of progress in the field and, therefore, a check on
the each new issue can prove fruitful.

Naturally, the continuous process of professional education
and of updating is crucial to remaining aware of what new
image sources are becoming available and which are either dis-
continued, no longer relevant or inappropriate. For this reason
and in this connection a large number of sources could be mentioned as impinging on the field of picture and slide collections.
Whereas their cumulative information would be great their individual contributions are quite slight. Patience and diligence is,
therefore, required on the part of the slide manager concerned in
this area of acquisition. It is usual that numerous sources will
need quick scanning rather than a few sources providing convenient and comprehensive detail.

A general overview of centres of activity is provided by *the
international yearbook of educational and training technology*. This is
useful for the latest address, telephone and functional details of
many of the academic, commercial and government-sponsored
bodies whose interests are concerned with image creation, storage and usage. Once more, however, the still image and the slide

is not the most prominent aspect, but critical use of this work is beneficial to the persistent searcher with a slide interest. Similarly the *Audio visual directory* has to be used with comparable discretion. Published annually by the producers of the monthly journal *Audiovisual* this work concentrates on the commercial world, covering audio-visual equipment manufacturers and suppliers, as well as producers of custom-made display and presentation support slides. The *Writers' and artists' yearbook* contains a useful list of picture libraries and agencies. The list makes clear in most cases whether a library specifically holds slides as a distinct format. The subject scope of the collections is also given in some detail. Indication is provided as to whether any particular library or agency is a member of the British Association of Picture Libraries and Agencies (BAPLA). The entries which are so designated can then be found in the Association's directory – (*BAPLA directory*) where more detailed information is provided. While neither list is or claims to be comprehensive, the *BAPLA directory* lists over 300 picture collections and when used in conjunction with the *yearbook*'s list, provides an effective coverage for the slide user. Furthermore, the annual production of both titles ensures currency. One could be forgiven for thinking that the *Libraries, museums and art galleries yearbook* (Brink, 1981) also appears on an annual basis, but publication is intermittent with the last edition being that of 1981 which covers the years 1978–79. A more dependable source, but with less direct slide information and covering another possible slide source group is the *Guide to government departments and other libraries*.

Although the slide holdings of medical libraries are listed, it should be noted that the preponderance of slides located within hospitals are held by departments of medical illustration not medical libraries. A list of departments of illustration can be found in the *Medical directory*, the *Medical Register* or *Hospitals and health service yearbook*. Another useful source of current information on the names of heads of departments of medical illustration and their precise working addresses is the membership list of the Institute of Medical and Biological Illustration (IMBI). The list is, however, of restricted circulation to affiliated members of IMBI and is unlikely to be freely accessible on the open shelves of libraries for instance. A good overview of the whole field is also available by referring to the *International guide to locating audio-visual materials in the health sciences*. More detail on specific libraries is given by the *Directory of medical and health care libraries in the UK and Republic of Ireland*. Although this work is published at irregular intervals, a new edition appears before the former edition has become too dated and a continuity of serviceable information is thereby maintained.

Audio-visual and slide provision in the medical and health care disciplines is so dominated and authoritatively provided for in the UK by the Graves Medical Audiovisual Library and their *UK National Medical Slide Bank* and the 'Slide Atlases' produced by Wolfe that the searcher hardly need look for other sources of supply. The Wolfe slides are published with comprehensive texts which include full details of clinical findings and relevant diagnoses in self-contained thematically arranged and indexed packages.

Searchers in the museums sphere are served by the *Bibliography of museum and art gallery publications and audiovisual aids in Great Britain and Northern Ireland* and by the *Catalog of museum publications and media* (Wasserman, 1980). The latter publication covers the US and Canada. The *Directory of British Photographic Collections* (Wall, 1977) though now dated was an ambitious project to collate information on almost all photographic formats held by collections ranging from those held by individuals to large nationally prominent institutions. Some ambiguity exists in the listings where the term transparency is used without the slide format size being provided.

Aimed at the professional picture researcher, but an equally useful reference aid for library acquisition purposes and public use are both *Picture sources UK* (Eakins, 1985) and its US counterpart *Picture sources 4* (Robl, 1983).

One source with a consistent reputation for accuracy and usefulness is the British Universities Film and Video Council (BUFVC) publication *Distributors: the guide to video and film sources for education and training* (Grant, 1990). Despite the subtitle details of slides are included in the subject arrangement which lists the catalogues of over 650 AVM suppliers of all sizes.

The BUFVC also maintains the database AVANCE which lists programmes including slide packages as part of the service to higher education.[3] The database succeeded the service known as HELPIS (Higher Education Learning Programme Information Service). The same organization provides an invaluable reference and information service for all matters audio-visual relating to higher education.

Another important publication again from the US, now in its 6th edition, is the *Slide buyers' guide* (Cashman, 1990). Unfortunately the UK lacks an equivalent publication to provide a more nationally-based focal point in an area which is both difficult for the beginner and frustrating for the more experienced acquisitions librarian. The *Slide buyers' guide* is, however, international in coverage as is the majority of the output of the Visual Resources Association and this makes the publication a fundamental and essential purchase for slide acquisition purposes.

Although a vitally important source, the *National directory of slide collections* (McKeown, 1990) does not aim to include commercial slide collections in its brief. Where a commercial interest is unclear the collection is included, but the bulk of entries are for public bodies, academic institutions, some from the medical field and such organizations as learned societies and professional institutions. Clearly, whereas this publication is not a list of slide supply sources in any direct sense it does embody the names and whereabouts of slide librarians with expertise in slide acquisition in the subject areas of their collections and to this extent is a valuable compilation of professional contacts. The publication represents fundamentally important research work in identifying the extent of slides as a national resource in the UK.

Mention should also be made of such independently administered projects as AXIS (The Visual Arts Exchange and Information service, Leeds Metropolitan University) and their publication *Visual arts information services handbook* which lists information sources and their slide holdings and availability. Although the majority of entries in the *ARLIS union list of microforms on art, design and related subjects* (Nichols, 1988), are for the microfiche format and consequently are of archival inspiration and interest, there are a number of entries which give details of colour material in 35mm reel (i.e. unmounted slide) form.

Also worthy of note and consultation is *World photography sources* (Bradshaw and Hahn, 1983). The searcher for slides needs to be aware that the foregoing sources should in many cases be approached with caution. In some of the above titles slides are by no means necessarily prominent. Entries, references or discussion relating to slides may be heavily obscured by material which only mentions slides obliquely or by implication and which is mainly devoted to the coverage of other audio-visual formats. It should be emphasized that this is the usual nature of the jungle through which the resolute slide seeker must try to cut a swath. Only by checking numerous sources and by constantly watching for new lists and publications can the slide manager hope to piece together a relatively complete jigsaw of the overall acquisition or slide supply picture. A number of the sources will indicate or direct the user to the relevant specialized supplier and the searcher must then move to the next stage of approaching the actual slide supplier obtaining the relevant listing/catalogues and compiling a range of current suppliers listings for the subject(s) of the collection being built or maintained.

Journals
A number of journals either deal directly with slides or have such a close association with them that commercial suppliers regularly use them as vehicles for advertising their stocks. General titles in this area are *Program* and the *Audiovisual Librarian*. In the visual arts field there is naturally a wide variety, the principal titles being the *Art Libraries Journal, Art Libraries News-sheet, Visual Resources: an international Journal of Documentation,* and *Computers in the history of art (CHART). Art Libraries News-sheet* is particularly outstanding as a current awareness source since it includes a regular section providing details of new slide sources and up-to-date information on established sources. The VRA bulletin is also invaluable since it contains a running update to the latest edition of the *Slide buyer's guide*. The BUFVC publishes the magazine *Viewfinder* three times a year which covers a wide range of interests in the film, television and related media including still images and slides.

In the museums area the Museum Documentation Association's *MDA Information* and the Museums' Association's *Museums News* are good sources and the general commercial sector is well covered by *Audio Visual, The British Journal of Photography* and the *BAPLA Journal*. In the specialized field of medicine the *Journal of Audiovisual Media in Medicine* and the newsletters of Graves Medical Audio Visual are pre-eminent.

Correspondence with or membership of appropriate professional bodies or subject interest groups can be a direct method of receiving the necessary information and journals listed above. The following list covers a selection of such organizations.

Organizations
ARLIS/UK AND EIRE (from 1993 ARLIS/UK and Ireland)
Visual Resources Group of ARLIS/NA
Library Association Audio Visual Group
Museums Documentation Association
Visual Resources Association (US)
Mid-America College Art Association (US)
British Association of Picture Libraries and Agencies
Society of Picture Researchers and Editors
British Universities Film and Video Council
National Art Slide Library and the Centre for Image Information
National Council for Educational Technology
Institute of Medical and Biological Illustration
Graves Medical Audio Visual Library

Naturally these bodies represent a large depository of advice and contacts of which the newcomer to a particular field can avail themselves. Further details can be found in the appendices.

4 The technical preparation of slides as stock items

The slide possesses inherent technical qualities purely as a photographic format which exist irrespective of whether or not the slide becomes a library item. The slide which does become part of library collection, however, has to undergo some technical library processing in order that it can be identified, retrieved and subsequently used as a visual information or library item. The slide manager must be aware of the photographic technicalities, but is unlikely to be involved in much resulting day-to-day activity thereafter, once a policy has been laid down. In the latter connection, however, concerning the routine processing of slides as part of the acquisition procedure, the slide manager has greater involvement in the preparatory work which converts a slide from possibly an anonymous entity into a valuable item of retrievable library stock.

Technical aspects of the slide – as a photographic format

The variety of slide format sizes was covered in the introductory chapter. Some other considerations are:

1   Whether archival master copies or other format copies are to be kept. It is now possible to consider the CD formats (particularly Photo-CD) as possible sources for backing up slide collections.

2   Atmospheric conditions.

3   Type of film to be used. This can involve film brand, type of base material and film speed preferred.

4   Cameras, lenses and other photographic equipment used by in-house sources. Quality conventional slide duplication equipment may be a considered investment, but again image databases and the CD formats provide another option.

5   In-house photographic processing – the extent and quality of facilities and staffing.

It cannot be ignored that slides have a limited life in comparison with many other library materials and an appreciable proportion of expenditure may be required to simply maintain a slide collection at a good quality level. It is only since as late as 1975 that widespread improvements in colour dyes have provided the prospect of preserving slide collections for a number of decades rather than only a few years. Stohlein writing in the 1970s estimated that the life of a well-used colour slide was only about six years.[1] Since that time, however, not only has the permanence of colour dyes been significantly improved, but film bases, particularly polyester, are more stable and absorb less moisture from the surrounding air and, therefore, deter the formation of fungi which attack the emulsion and obscure the picture. The principal

sources recommend a storage temperature for slides not exceed-
ing 21° C (70° F) and a relative humidity of between 30 and 40 per
cent. The almost common-sense conditions of constant temperature and a dry, dust free atmosphere are also mentioned by most
sources. Such provisions apply to working collections. It is
recommended that slides stored purely for preservation, in
archives, are maintained at a temperature of 0° C or slightly
below freezing. Naturally, special care has to be taken when
extracting slides from such conditions into warmer surround-
ings where heavy condensation is likely to be immediately
deposited on the slides if the temperature rise is too abrupt.

It is not difficult to appreciate that the conditions a slide experiences when it is projected are not conducive to preservation.
The temperature during projection can become considerable
despite the cooling fans of projectors. It is important to be aware
that the white slide of a slide mount is designed to reflect away
the heat of projection and should always face the projection bulb
when the slide is in the projector. Clearly, the less time a slide is
projected the better its chances of being preserved or not suffer-
ing the deleterious effects described, but such considerations can
hardly be placed above effective reasonable use of the informa-
tion/learning resources. High temperatures during projection or
raised temperature levels during storage reduce the pliability of
film bases and accelerate the fading of colour dyes. Low humidity (over-dry conditions) can also cause brittleness of film bases
whereas high humidity promotes the problems associated with
moisture. Although normal office lighting will not lead to the
fading of slide dyes, the power of sunlight should never be
underestimated. Slides accidently left on a window sill, for
example, in strong summer sun can be badly faded in hours and
it is essential that borrowers are aware of this vulnerability.

Unfortunately when slides are acquired through purchase it is
not possible to ensure that the film used or the other qualities of
the slide are of the best type for prolonged use. Efforts have been
made particularly in the US by the VRA and other bodies (e.g.
Mid-America College Art Association) to positively influence
suppliers by publishing required standards on slide quality.
Clearly, greater control can be exercised over the production of

slides when they are created by the parent organization. This can extend to employing professional photographic staff who require no training in the selection of camera equipment or the appropriate film for a particular assignment or need. It is not the purpose here to provide technical details of slide film. Such information is available from standard texts on photography or from the technical data sheets of such prominent manufacturers as Kodak or Ilford.[2] A wealth of technical specifications can be obtained from these sources on, for example, films which are colour corrected for use under different lighting types and conditions. The work of Tull and more particularly Sundt is essential reading in this area.[3]

Technical aspects of the slide – as a library item for acquisitions processing

The mounting of slides

The type of slide mount used, clearly has implications for the preservation of the photographic image. Since lantern slides employed glass as a base material onto which the light sensitive emulsion was coated, it was logical to protect this surface with another sheet of glass following exposure. Binding between glass continued as other film bases became available, eventually to be followed by patented slide mounts. In the 1950s the introduction of modern pliable and durable plastic mounts provided for greater convenience since the mouldings were designed to hold the actual film precisely on locating points and for the two halves of the mount to press and hold exactly together without the need for additional adhesives or securing.

Many commercially-produced, budget-priced slides were and continue to be mounted in cardboard. Although it is possible to retain these mounts for images which receive only occasional or very careful use, it is not to be recommended, since such mounts are subject to wear and to bending or being accidently crushed. In addition the lightweight nature of cardboard mounts can lead to them not falling precisely into the projection gate during use. Anything technically based which prejudices the smooth running of lectures or the trouble free use of slides should be elimi-

nated as far as possible at the processing stage and for these reasons cardboard mounts are to be discouraged. It is the case that
cardboard mounts are in many cases clearly and attractively
printed with much essential or useful information and it is
unfortunate that this feature has to be destroyed to improve the
durability of the image. Naturally the relevant information has
to be preserved by transcribing the details to accession and cataloguing records.

When cardboard mounts have been rejected the choice
remains between plastic mounts which are either glassless or
which incorporate glass within the mount. Often available
funds, or lack of them, will decide the issue since glass mounts
are appreciably more expensive. Obviously if a slide is mounted
in a glassless mount the slide surface remains exposed to the
atmosphere, dust, finger deposits and possible scratching.
Furthermore, when projected the film is more directly exposed
to the heat of projection and the air flow created by the projector's fan. The heat of projection leads to a differential expansion
of the base and emulsion sides of the slide. This results in the film
forming a curve or bulge. The projected image can thus sud-
denly snap out of focus (commonly referred to as 'popping') as
the film changes curvature, and this can prove disruptive to the
projection process. Attempts to eliminate this effect have been
made by introducing mounts which impose an initial bulge or
curve on the slide in its 'cold' or pre-projection state, thereby
minimizing the degree of further movement.

Mounting slides between glass prevents movement of the film
surface and thus eliminates popping, but mounting must be carried out in a dry atmosphere to preclude the possibility of moisture being trapped within the mount. Newly-processed film can
contain a residual quantity of moisture and care should be taken
to allow the material to dry out. Moisture in a slide mount, in
addition to furthering fungal growth, can lead to the emulsion
adhering to the glass surface. Subsequent cleaning or remount-
ing of the image will then be rendered impossible since when the
old mount is opened the emulsion will tear away from the film-
base material. The phenomenon known as 'Newton's rings'
which manifests itself as a circular spectrum or rainbow pattern

superimposed on the image has been attributed to both the presence of moisture and to a perfect contact being achieved between the film surface and the glass. Anti-Newton ring mounts possess a matt surface on the side of the glass which comes into contact with film.

In general terms slide collections mounted in glassless slides have proved workable, in well-used collections, especially where it is impressed upon users not to handle the surface of a slide. In one sense mounting slides in glass can indirectly encourage touching of the picture area of a slide because users feel that it is protected. However, the accumulated finger deposits on the glass can lead to a sticky surface which attracts further dirt. It can be a feature of glass mounts that they require more cleaning than glassless mounted slides. A thin, oily deposit can build up on the glass surface without it being immediately obvious and the dull appearance of an image can be assumed unconsciously to be due to the age of the image rather than the progressively acquired dirt. Any cleaning carried out on slides mounted in glassless mounts naturally involves cleaning the actual delicate emulsion or film-base surfaces. Methylated spirit is the preferred agent for cleaning. The high volatility of this substance ensures that the base material does not absorb any of the liquid. Some sources recommend the final bath of slide processing chemical as a cleaning or washing agent and others mention distilled water.

Any cleaning process for slides is a time-consuming process and prevention is always preferable to cure. The utmost care has to be taken to avoid any abrasive action on the slide surface. This particularly applies to the emulsion which can quickly become detached from the film base destroying the image irretrievably. Gentle use of cotton buds is possibly the best method, but no rubbing or pressure can be employed. The dissolving action of the methylated spirit must be allowed to effect the cleaning rather than the action of wiping. The cotton should be thoroughly soaked in order to prevent the cotton itself becoming a contaminant.

Where large numbers of slide acquisitions are involved, machine mounting should be investigated. Such machines can cut and mount whole films in one automatic process and have obvious benefits in the saving of staff time for large operations.

Finally, as mentioned previously, it is important that the white half of a plastic mount forms the front of the finished slide since this face is designed to maximize the reflection of unwanted heat during projection.

Labelling

The labelling of slides in structured collections has traditionally been a somewhat neglected aspect of slide management. Legible, consistent and attractive printed labelling can make a marked difference to the efficient use of a collection, the discipline of retrieval and from a public relations view point the image the collection wishes to project (no puns intended!).

A collection which buys slides from a wide variety of sources is likely to be presented with as many methods and types of labelling. While many will provide full and useful information, it is tempting to retain this in the form received. However, to do this consistency will have to be sacrificed and the information is unlikely to be in the arrangement or form preferred. Furthermore, in a classified collection the purchase slide will need the addition of the all-important classification number and an accession number. The widespread adoption of automated management methods for slide collections has provided the opportunity to create custom-made, consistently laid out labels which with small typefaces maximize the limited area available on mounts. All the necessary information can of course be selected from the accessions or catalogue database entry and printed without the need for any additional typing process.

Manual systems often lead to inconsistency and the adoption of disparate labelling both from external suppliers and in-house. Although microtypeface typewriters created satisfactory results this is an additional library process and introduced another possibility of human error and inconsistency between the cataloguing record and the label. Most slide mounts now have a matt surface which is suitable for handwritten labelling with a felt-tip pen. Although this may be useful for the amateur or home-based slide user it is not recommended in the professionally organized and automated slide library. While it is no longer difficult to obtain labels of appropriate dimensions to fit slide mounts the adhesives should be checked to ensure they do not peel away from the mount as a result of normal wear or the heat of projection. The best quality adhesive properties are required for labels which are intended to remain in place for the life of the slide.

Orientation

Of the eight ways of placing a slide in a projector, only one is correct. It is, therefore, desirable for convenience, particularly when dealing quickly with numerous slides to indicate the correct orientation of a slide.

An adhesive spot of a prominent colour should be stuck at the bottom left-hand corner of the front of the mounted slide when the illustration is viewed in its correct attitude. When placed in the projector the slide is turned through 180 degrees so that the same spot is at the top right. The inversion of the image is necessary to compensate for the inversion imposed by the projector lens. Such an indicator is of course of value for viewing for selection purposes directly from storage. Normally for the majority of images it will be obvious which way up is correct, but for some technical matter and artwork the correct placing of the indicator could be the only subsequent method of determining the correct orientation.

The other category of slides which can prove particularly awkward, not to say galling, to handle without orientation indication are those where the longer side of the slide forms the vertical (often referred to as the portrait format). It is essential that the orientation of slides is correct in storage as well as for projection.

Many working collections of slides have overlooked or neglected this aspect of slide management by not consistently ensuring that orientation indicators are affixed to slides.

35mm full frame slide – 2 × 2 inch frame (Actual size)

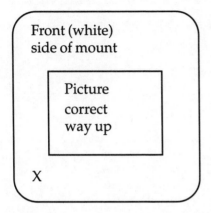

X = Adhesive indicator of correct way up for projection.

Figure 1   Orientation indicator on slide

The slide is inverted when projected, so that the indicator spot is visible when the slide is inserted in, for example, a Kodak Carousel slide magazine.

5   Slide retrieval

Introduction

Although in one sense it is accepted that libraries or library systems are in their entirety, retrieval systems, it is usual to refer more narrowly to cataloguing, classification and indexing as a 'library's retrieval system'. This dual use or different levels of use of the word retrieval can be confusing and needs some clarification. This is important when referring to slide libraries, since these aspects of slide management are interwoven and so closely influence each other that they cannot be separated successfully. Both the broader use of the term retrieval system – to refer to either the whole library (or slide library), or the narrower use to refer exclusively to cataloguing, classification and indexing have useful applications. Normally it is clear from the context when the broader or narrower sense is being used, but it is helpful to be conscious of the particular sense being employed when considering slide library management.

To summarize, the term retrieval in the broad sense covers:

1   The overall process of finding the stored slides including interaction with the users, defining their requirements and advising on how to locate the slides required.
2   The storage system.
3   The arrangement within storage.
4   The classification system.
5   The cataloguing.
6   The indexing.

The narrower usage of the term covers 4-6.

Using a classified arrangement

The whole slide library organization and processes designed to benefit the user, which consist of the type of physical storage method for the slides, their arrangement within that storage and their cataloguing, classification and indexing, in combination, form the components of the broad use of the term retrieval system. It can be seen that this wider use of the term embraces the narrower usage and it is immediately apparent that the adoption of a subject classification scheme for both the arrangement of the slides in storage and as an element in the cataloguing record forges a 'finding link' between the actual pictorial information (i.e. the physical slide file) and the text of the cataloguing record whether it is recorded manually or electronically.

Slides in storage (subject classified arrangement)

link to

Cataloguing record (includes subject classification number)

Retrieval file in classified order – if manual system is used this is usually on 5 × 3 inch cards.

Search by classification number/heading if automated system.

Should it be decided to create a self-indexing collection it remains necessary to choose an appropriate arrangement order. The arrangement becomes the principal or perhaps the only retrieval device and assumes greater importance in the absence of separate cataloguing records or independent indexes. This is not to say that there may not be catalogue details interfiled with the slides when a self-indexing collection is housed in an appropriate storage system which allows this.

It is instructive and should be noted from this how the choice of one aspect of slide management interlocks with other choices and leads to an effective overall system which is appropriate to the user, the staffing situation, the budget and size and purpose of the collection. Clearly the opposite is true and inconsistent choices can produce a disjointed system where the retrieval components are incongruous and do not combine well to maximize efficiency. Indeed it is possible that one type of feature may partially or wholly negate the value of another. Some of the problems in this connection will be covered later.

If a subject classified arrangement is not adopted, however (whether the collection is to be self-indexing or not), then the finding link referred to above will need to be made by an unclassified arrangement order.

The subject classification adopted can be:

1 A published scheme using notation (usually numeric).
2 A locally-developed scheme.
3 A non-library scheme adapted from another discipline, e.g. statistics.
4 A system of controlled alphabetical subject headings. This can either be a published list such as Sear's List of Subject Headings, the Library of Congress list, *Art and Architecture Thesarus* or a locally-developed thesaurus.

Published classification schemes

General and specialized schemes
The relative merits of enumerative and faceted classifications (and of alphabetical subject headings) are well covered by

authoritative sources[1] and it is not necessary to cover them here in detail. By far the most familiar published enumerative classification scheme is the Dewey Decimal Classification (DDC), currently in its 20th edition.[2] The scheme's widespread use, particularly by public but also by other libraries, and its easily followed numerical shelf order has secured such an established place for the scheme that it is now unlikely to be displaced. However, since slide collections composed of single images are self-contained and separate from other library collections it is not normally necessary to use the same classification as is employed for other major collections within a library, such as the book stock. It may of course be appropriate to use the scheme already in use in other parts of the same organization particularly if this is helpful to users, but no such compulsion exists. It is, therefore, advisable not to automatically opt for the Dewey scheme as a first reaction, but to consider other schemes which may be more appropriate to the subject coverage of a given collection.

For a general subject, multidisciplinary or specialist slide collections the Universal Decimal Classification (UDC) is worthy of consideration.[3] The scheme has separate subject schedules of greater refinement than Dewey as well as a schedule for general collections (BS1000M: Part 1: 1985). The schedules appropriate to the subject and the depth of the collection can, therefore, be chosen as they relate to any specific collection. UDC also has the inherent ability to specify very specialized subjects. For example in the medical field there are separate sections for anatomy, orthopaedics, pathology and other branches of biomedical knowledge.

It is useful to briefly and fundamentally compare the application of a classification scheme with a system of alphabetical subject headings as methods for determining the arrangement of the slides. With respect to alphabetical subject headings it is acknowledged that large systems can become cumbersome if subdivisions are used and the principle objection is that such arrangements of natural language headings juxtapose subjects according to their arbitrary place in the alphabet rather than in a helpful subject order throughout. It is further recognized that the usual remedy for this – the inversion of headings – while grouping together like subjects, leads to the creation and use of 'unsought terms' or headings which are unlikely to be any user's immediate thought when searching. These headings are, therefore, unlikely to be obvious approaches to the visual information. Elaborate systems of references also have to be added to guide the user, and this again increases the size of the file without the user going directly to the information required. One of the foremost and successful systems for resolving some of these difficulties has been the Preserved Context Indexing System (PRECIS) (see Austin, 1984)[4] which has been used for a number of years to provide subject indexing for the British National Bibliography (BNB). By rotating terms in the indexing phrase or string, in a controlled and edited manner, many more entry points are generated in preference to additional references and the user has more direct access to the information. The natural consequence of this is that the index is long and automated methods have been developed to rotate the indexing terms according to the indexers wishes for each string.[5] A powerful method of providing retrieval for slides would be to use PRECIS in conjunction with a classification scheme, but there appears to be no example of this in practice or in any report.

A suitable notational classification scheme, however, provides the classifier and user with a logical order and control, by placing the desired associated subjects together in the scheme. This is not to say that notational schemes do not have their limitations since any physical, linear sequence of items cannot group together all the subjects as is ideally required and inevitably some subjects are scattered and appear in more than one place in the collection. Also many of the well-established enumerative schemes, the prominent example being the Dewey Decimal Classification, have drawbacks related to their age. As the state and growth of knowledge has progressed the relationships between subjects and their relative disproportionate growth has created anomalies within such systems which regular revision has not altogether been able to counter. Furthermore, the rapid change of knowledge in some areas makes it difficult for new editions to keep pace. It is evident that there is no ideal method of classification and compromise and balanced judgements are always necessary to achieve effective results.

On balance, however, an appropriate notational subject classification is desirable, in principle, as a first choice, for the majority of slide libraries, and the shorthand aspect of the notational representation of a subject is both easier to fit on to the limited space afforded by a slide mount and perhaps easier to file precisely in the storage arrangement. As always the greater degree of definition or refinement that is applied using a subject classification leads to numbers of increasing length and a compromise needs to be reached between the level of subject refinement and the convenience of number length. It is clearly not desirable to use a general classification for a specialized collection without some adaptation or editing as this can lead to inordinately lengthy numbers, many of which will begin with the same repetitious number and be unhelpful to the user and cumbersome to administer. A useful technique to edit Dewey numbering and economically adapt it or indeed other schemes to a particular collection is to add an alphabetical prefix or suffix as required of up to three letters. Whereas a prefix can be used to create major initial categories, suffixes can be used to subdivide.

Despite the merits of using a classification, it must not be overlooked that an alphabetical subject index is required to guide the user from a natural language subject enquiry to its notational representation (i.e. the classification number) in the scheme and its place in the storage sequence. However, the growing use of automated methods can lead to a satisfactory resolution of many of the drawbacks of using natural language subject-terms mentioned above.

The picture and slide classification scheme of Simons and Tansey has been discussed in Chapter 2 on literature. Clearly, when choosing a classified arrangement for slides this work should be examined before a final choice is made. Not only is the scheme useful in its possible application, but the introduction is instructive to slide managers whether or not the scheme itself is adopted. Wright's comparative discussion and criticism of this scheme and others is also invaluable.[6] General schemes tend to be widely used in a variety of book and picture collections and are, therefore, well maintained and kept up to date by regularly issued new editions. Specialist schemes on the other hand are often smaller-scale publishing enterprises or originate from a narrower base, possibly from a single specialist organization. However, such organizations are usually large, influential and significant in their own subject field. In the visual arts field, institutions which have developed their own classifications worthy of special note are, in the UK the Courtauld Institute of Art and in the US the scheme of the Harvard Fine Arts Library, the Harvard Fogg Art Museum Photograph and Slide Library and related scheme of the New York Metropolitan Museum of Art Photograph and Slide Library.

Also mentioned in Chapter 2, the ICONCLASS scheme is available to the fine arts slide librarian, but the approach of the scheme is based on the discipline of iconography rather than the primary subject matter usually used for cataloguing visual arts library materials.

The specialized schemes which apply to the medical subject field are discussed in Chapter 7. In the building area the CI/SfB scheme is applicable and should be reviewed in this connection.[7]

Locally developed schemes

Developing an in-house classification scheme for a particular slide collection is a positive decision which requires careful consideration of a number of detailed points before a sound decision can be taken. The natural advantage of doing this and the overriding reason why such a course of action should be undertaken will be that the resulting classification will, at least initially, be coextensive and relate exactly to the subject content of the collection. It is necessary to appreciate the amount of learning, research, reading and time to compile a new classification which must not only cover the existing collection, but anticipate developments and be flexible enough to accommodate change. It is more often than not the case that a subject discipline or area is either included in some existing broader classification or that there exists some structuring of knowledge published for use in another connection which relates to the collection to be classified. These possibilities are covered in the next section and such options should be fully explored before embarking on the creation of a new scheme.

The steps necessary to devise a classification are:

1   Define the existing and likely future subject extent of the collection.

2   Ascertain the present and eventual likely upper limit of the working collection.

3   Analyse a sample number of user requirements and enquiries and gauge the depth of subject specificity required.

4   Consider this in the context of whether the collection is general or highly specialized.

5   Decide on the main classes and how many there are to be.

6   Determine any common characteristics which slides may have despite being in different main classes.

7   Devise a suitable alphabetical or numerical notation.

Subject lists which can be used for arrangement order
The medical field is particularly rich in classifications and subject lists which, while not designed specifically for pictorial material, do provide systematic arrangements of subject matter:

Excerpta medica
Medical Subject Headings (MeSH) (Index Medicus)
International Classification of Diseases (ICD) (WHO)
Standard nomenclature of diseases and operations
Systematized nomenclature of medicine (SnoMed)
Systematized nomenclature of pathology (SNOP)

These are the more prominent titles and they are discussed further in Chapter 7.

The validity of applying book classifications to slides and how the technological development has affected the choices

Arguments have been put forward which claim that book classifications are inappropriate for the classification of pictorial material. In essence the arguments appear to be based on the fact that pictorial material depicts concrete entities only and is unable to deal with abstract concepts. Subjects such as psychology, religion, literature, poetry and music or doctrines, beliefs, theories and institutions cannot be directly illustrated although they can be represented symbolically. This has led to attempts to devise special classification schemes to cater exclusively for pictures. The fact that a picture is always of an object created at some point in time past has also been a starting-point for new classification schemes using initially a theoretical approach based on the picture purely as a historical record. In opposition to this it has been pointed out that it is only necessary and perfectly workable to ignore or simply not to use the parts of a book classification which have no application for pictures and slides.[8] This seems a commonsense solution especially for the practising slide manager who generally does not have time to consider, over deeply, the theories, which are unlikely to be productive in an everyday situation. Much of the work referred to above was carried out before microcomputers of sufficient power and competitive cost were available to be considered for retrieval systems in the typical picture or slide library. While much of the theory about the retrieval of pictorial information was sound, interesting and instructive it did not appear to make any significant impact on how pictorial information is managed in practice in libraries. No new special classification or indexing methods emerged or found widespread adoption and it was rather the methods from general information management which continued to be adapted and improvised for the needs of picture management.

However, the introduction of the new technology at an ever-increasing rate of change has largely taken such considerations out of the hands of the slide manager who will increasingly in the future be far more concerned with purchasing the most appropriate automated picture or database management system than with creating a sound theoretically-based system as was the case not long ago when manual techniques were the only choice. The power of database management systems, multimedia and of the compact disc (CD) to store and retrieve pictures is such that deliberations over classifications of slides in storage will have a reduced significance since single or multiple images will be retrieved and displayed on screen in fractions of a second. Nevertheless, whatever the future brings in revolutionizing picture use and retrieval, existing valuable physical files of slides will have to dovetail with the new technologies in such a way that they are efficient to use. Many slide files remain original source material which the new technologies will make all the more easy to copy, store and retrieve. The most likely situation for the foreseeable future is the co-existence of conventionally-produced photographic images of all types and the newer electronic produced images. Conventional photography using the 35mm format in particular is so well established in so many areas that it is difficult to see it being rapidly displaced and it is likely that the creation of images by conventional methods will persist even if those images are subsequently stored, manipulated and incorporated in CD and computer systems or other picture systems yet to be developed. This is not to underestimate the power of CD and other electronic picture storage systems to radically change how picture collections are stored, managed and used, but it is unwise to prejudge the implications when the rate of change is so rapid and apparently ever increasing.

A parallel can perhaps be drawn with the predictions some years ago when it was suggested by some sources that widespread adoption of computers would lead to the 'paperless office' and the diminution of conventional book publishing. The reality was that the computer complemented existing systems rather than rendered them obsolete. Whereas the process of typesetting for instance was revolutionized and hot metal methods superseded, the end product – the newspaper, for example, remained viable and competitive both commercially and culturally. By analogy the ability of the new CD-based picture systems not only to store pictures (and slides) in perfect condition, but allow them to be reproduced in their original format may lead to more rather than less conventional slides being generated in the future. If so, such a development would mirror progress in the office which far from being paperless has now to manage greater quantities of print created by computer output.

Pronouncements that the slide is obsolete are premature. It is significant that the new developments such as CD are storage rather than creative devices, and that conventional photography remains the principal creative source of high-definition pictures. A greater threat to the slide's continuance is likely to come about when high-resolution pictures are generated in greater profusion by video and by the electronic 'filmless' camera and computer graphics. This, coupled with high-definition colour television, as a standard feature, is likely to have a greater effect on the present dominance and future regress of conventional photography. At present, however, advances appear to be greater in the technologies concerned with picture storage rather than creation. For libraries such advances are centred, at least for the moment on the standard microcomputers and the CD-ROM drive peripheral.

The importance of the choice between a classified or an unclassified arrangement

To return to classification, however, the decision to adopt a classified arrangement and to classify each slide individually may at first appear a daunting and to some an over-elaborate undertaking. Yet the fact of the matter is that the overall value of a slide collection composed of single images is finally dependent on having the capability to retrieve any individual image and all relevant images for which any user may have need. Only by a system which devotes detailed attention to individual images at the input stage will it be possible to provide for these needs at the point of request and delivery. Naturally, there are always exceptions, abbreviated methods and economies which apply to special collections and circumstances, but such decisions will always be a balanced judgement made locally by individual slide collection managers. Furthermore, if an automated system is used, the return on the attention paid to detailed work at the input stage is more than repaid at the output stage when the system is able to comprehensively answer the demands made by users.

For the librarian familiar with assigning a classification number to the substantial body of information contained in a book, the slide may appear a rather slight entity by comparison. An initial reaction may be that such a small item cannot justify the labour involved in individual classification. Clearly, it is necessary for librarians to be detached and objective about slide retrieval if they are to remain unprejudiced about the necessary methods which may need to be applied to manage a slide collection.

Whether or not to employ a classified arrangement is possibly the key decision of slide management and retrieval. If it can be said that there is a starting point in the management of a slide collection, then making this decision is possibly such a place for beginning the planning and design of a slide retrieval system. If, for example, the decision to buy a particular storage system is taken without first deciding on the arrangement order then it may be found impossible to subsequently introduce a classified arrangement. Any storage system which does not allow for slides to be interfiled eliminates the option of a classified arrangement since the interfiling of new additions into the collection is a prerequisite to maintaining a subject order for the material when using a classification scheme or indeed an alphabetical arrangement. It is almost impossible to make changes either from a classified to a running number order or vice versa once a particular arrangement has been introduced. Such change would effectively mean physically reorganizing a collection and this is unlikely to be a realistic option in most practical working situations. Where it is considered to be a possibility it is hardly one which is likely to be relished.

If a classification is to be used then this is likely to directly determine or strongly impinge upon:

1   The storage arrangement.

2   A cataloguing detail and retrieval approach, i.e. search by class number.

3   The type of storage system used – since not all systems allow interfiling of new material which a classified arrangement demands.

4   The extent of the browsing capabilities of the collection. The classification will group certain subjects, but will inevitably scatter others. This is likely to directly influence users' choices and their approach to the images by determining the proximity of like images in storage. The manager may need to make judicious adjustments to a scheme to meet local circumstances.

5   The nature of the indexing. Should subject index entries be generated from the classification scheme then it will also directly determine this aspect of retrieval.

In the light of considering the central importance of the classified arrangement as a priority in slide libraries it is now necessary to assess the relative merits of the storage methods available. However, it will be necessary to return to consider in more detail the other possibilities for the arrangement of slides in storage in unclassified arrangements.

Methods of storage

As stated above the method chosen for the storage of slides in a structured collection is fundamental in the effects this will have on many aspects of slide retrieval and in particular on what this decision will permit during actual practical usage.

The storage method directly affects how the users initially perceive the collection and it will actually determine or strongly influence the way in which they will use the collection and have access to the stock. Unlike many other audio-visual materials the slide does not require the close proximity of much sophisticated technical equipment for the medium to be quickly accessed and appreciated, a simple light box will suffice. Video and audio tapes, for example, are totally inert media without the necessary playback machinery, whereas pictorial material and the slide, once located in a collection, are more immediately approachable and useable. It can be further argued that pictures are even more easily accessible than print material since some of the necessary 'picture literacy' skills are more naturally acquired in infancy and usually precede formal reading and writing skills. This inherent immediacy of access, and the suitability for browsing, image comparison and scanning, which the slide possesses can either be recognized and furthered by the choice of storage system or can go unrecognized and even be consciously ignored and thus lost. The latter course of action in most situations is an unnecessary waste of a natural attribute which the slide possesses and it is unlikely to be desirable to allow this to happen without good reason in the majority of slide collections. Any slide storage system that involves a physical interposition between the user and the transparency, or demands a fixed and inflexible arrangement order which in turn precludes interfiling or provides no physical protection against handling during the time when slides are being selected is, therefore, undesirable. Since slide collections can grow inexorably from nothing, a storage system which does not allow for expansion is also likely to prove unhelpful and also ultimately becomes unworkable. By planning ahead most, if not all, of these problems can be avoided at the time when a collection is established. Quite often storage systems exhibit one or more of the drawbacks mentioned above.

Specific storage methods

Six main slide storage methods will be covered here. There are other variants, but in any event a system will be judged mainly by the following criteria.

These cover the extent to which a storage system provides for:

1   The interfiling of new material.
2   Substantial expansion of the collection.
3   Direct visual access to the images and close proximity of a light source.
4   Easy browsing, scanning and comparison of images.
5   Physical protection for the slides.
6   Competitive cost per unit slide.

These criteria are not listed here in order of importance. In practical terms it would be useful for individual managers to rearrange the list in the order they judge to be most applicable to their respective collections.

The six storage methods are:

1 Projector magazines.
2 Adapted catalogue drawers.
3 Purpose-designed slide cabinets with slotted drawers.
4 Purpose-made slide files.
5 Plastic wallets/sleeves with pockets kept in ring binders.
6 Plastic wallets/sleeves with pockets kept in filing cabinets.

Projector magazines
Although it may initially appear an attractive idea for reasons of convenience to store slides in projector magazines it is not generally desirable and ultimately may become unworkable as a system applied to a large collection of slides managed as single images. The method is possibly more appropriate to a medium-sized collection of tape/slide sequences or a finite collection of slide sets where the slides form fixed programmes which are repeatedly used without rearrangement.

Furthermore, the magazines themselves require storage and this can prove problematical particularly if the more commonly available rotary magazines are used, which normally hold 80 slides. A large amount of floor and shelf space is required for the number of slides stored and also the cost of this form of storage is high and easy access to individual slides for browsing is made more difficult. On the positive side this form of storage provides almost ideal protection for the slide surface and is highly efficient for immediate and convenient projection with the minimum of preparation. Although circumstances can be imagined where the balance of advantages against disadvantages of using projector magazines is such that this method can be gainfully adopted, the likely application is for a collection where flexible usage of the slides is not required and, therefore, cataloguing and indexing is minimal or possibly only listings of the slides in their fixed sequences are provided. Such special circumstances could exist in, for example, a small collection allied to a lecture theatre in a specialized subject area, repeatedly used by a few lecturers regularly delivering the same set of lectures in circumstances which require rapid preparation of the slides as an audio-visual aid. As outlined earlier, however, such a special case is not the primary case with which this book is concerned or with which the majority of slide managers are faced. The more usual situation is a structured collection of single images which need to be organized flexibly to meet an almost infinite number of different user requirements within the subject scope of the collection. Storage of slides in projector magazines is perhaps the least helpful method of furthering the aims of such a collection.

Adapted catalogue drawers and purpose-designed slotted drawers

The general progress in libraries from manual to automated cataloguing methods has led to the obsolescence of many traditional wooden cabinets designed to hold securely often several thousands of 5 × 3 inch catalogue cards. This type of furniture was and is usually manufactured to high cabinet-making standards and was a substantial capital item at the time of purchase. Naturally, before disposing of such an asset, which has little resale value, the prudent information manager is likely to look for possible new uses for what some would consider attractive furniture, particularly when plastic is replacing solid wood in many library and office environments. It is fortuitous indeed that such a specialized piece of furniture whose drawers were specifically designed for 5 × 3 inch cards should conveniently accommodate two parallel rows of 2 × 2 inch slides.

It is, therefore, logical and wise in times of financial stringency for libraries to be resourceful in this way and consider the reuse of card cabinets for slide storage. The method does not, however, allow for the interfiling of new material in a convenient way or for the indefinite expansion of the collection. Moving large numbers of slides from drawer to drawer is not easily carried out. While physical protection for the slides is reasonably well-catered for, it does not equal the protection provided by plastic sleeves, for example. As users examine the file and thumb through the slides, they invariably handle many slides which they are unlikely or do not wish to use and this wear and tear can be destructive if the collection is heavily used and the slides are not mounted between glass. The very action of extracting and refiling can lead to wear on the slides immediately adjacent to the slide required. Direct visual access is adequate, but the housing does not permit the easy comparison of images. Although a light source may by conveniently sited nearby, each slide has to be individually extracted from the file for viewing. Unit cost may be kept low, but some thought needs to be applied to adapting the drawers so that the slides will remain upright and in an orderly sequence. This is usually carried out by inserting a wooden or cardboard divider both along the centre length of the drawer and at intervals in the slide sequence, but this does not always avoid slides falling flat when a sequence of slides is removed for loan and in these circumstances some adjustable support for the slides is desirable.

One distinct advantage of storing slides in former card-catalogue cabinets is that when the collection is self-indexing and there are no separate retrieval devices, the housing allows card dividers to indicate subject or other divisions. Again the dimensions of the drawers permits cards to project above the slide height by up to an inch and ample room for extensive typed descriptive and guiding information can be achieved. It is possible for each card to have its own typed information card filed adjacent to it giving comprehensive details of the illustration, whether it is present in the file or when it is absent on loan.

Much of the above which applies to adapted catalogue drawers can also equally apply to purpose-made commercially available slotted drawers. These are normally manufactured in sheet steel similar to standard filing cabinets with plastic inlaid trays in the drawers. The plastic is moulded into slots designed to hold 2 × 2 inch slides in a vertically upright position at narrowly-spaced intervals. This facilitates the removal of individual slides without touching adjacent slides and this is an advantage over adapted catalogue drawers. However, the slides cannot be directly viewed from their position in storage and their removal during selection is obligatory. This can make browsing a laborious undertaking and be a serious drawback when it is required to compare images arranged in classified order. Again interfiling of new material is difficult and the method of storage is not as efficient at space saving as it may first appear. As a collection expands it can lead to the constant need to purchase new cabinets. Cabinets usually hold between 2,000 and 5,500 slides. The purpose-made slotted files do not have the advantage of the adapted catalogue drawers of being able to accommodate guide cards or other typed insertions and, therefore, the self-indexing possibilities are not readily available.

Purpose-made slide files

Perhaps the most imposing systems of slide storage are those employing purpose-designed cabinets. Naturally these are expensive, are manufactured to a high standard of wood laminate finish and house the slide stock in secure trays or racks which open over an in-built colour corrected light source. In the larger and more sophisticated models the light sources switch on and off automatically when either drawers are opened or slide racks withdrawn for viewing. They are free-standing pieces of furniture which are lockable. In a commercial situation where it is good business to create an atmosphere of well-appointed efficiency this is perhaps the most appropriate form of storage. Although the units are expensive, they are compact, afford good protection for the slides and browsing is an integral part of the product design. Unless further units are bought the system does not provide easily for expansion. Whereas other systems provide the means for gradual or incremental expansion, this method requires the purchase of a sizeable unit which in turn commits the manager to both a considerable new usage of floor space and to the incorporation of a unit which is likely to initially greatly exceed the medium term needs for expansion. The larger units house no more than 20,000 slides and appear to be designed more for the commercial/professional photographic world rather than the lending library serving a large parent institution. The systems are, however, most likely to find use in a heavily-used, prestigious or specialized collection which is unlikely to expand greatly or where slides are constantly renewed and the overall total stock figure remains largely unchanged.

Plastic sleeves in ring binders and plastic sleeves in filing cabinets

For many years transparent plastic sleeves have been commercially available which are composed of a number of pockets each of which holds a 2×2 inch slide. A wide variety of sleeves are manufactured by photographic suppliers to accommodate the needs of professional and amateur photographers and slide libraries. The differing sleeves are designed not only to hold slides, but also negatives, prints of all sizes, accompanying booklets or other printed material and audio cassettes. For slide library purposes two sizes are most commonly used. The A4 size sleeve holding 20 slides in five rows of four pockets is designed to fit into a standard ring binder and has the necessary moulded holes in the sheet to make this possible. The second size is designed to fit into a standard filing cabinet, holds 24 slides in four rows of six pockets and is supplied with a metal bar from which each sleeve is suspended within the filing cabinet.

The convenience of keeping slides either in ring binders or filing cabinets, both of which are standard and flexibly used office items, makes this method of storage an obvious choice in many working situations. In addition, no other method provides as good a combination of advantages. The slides are well protected during browsing yet easily visible for scanning or comparison without removal of the individual slides from the sleeve, thus avoiding direct handling of the slide surface. If a classified arrangement is used then new material is easily inserted in the storage sequence and stock moved to another drawer to maintain even spacing. Additionally a collection using these methods of storage can be expanded easily and the degree of expansion can be controlled. Whereas it would be usual to purchase a four-drawer filing cabinet when expansion is necessary, if smaller increases are expected then double or single cabinets can be obtained as necessary. Coupled with the above advantages and the competitive cost per unit slide, this form of storage is very popular in libraries and information units where funds are limited yet where a steady gradual growth is expected.

Since their first appearance plastic sleeves have been perfected to become something of a standard or first choice method for slide storage and they are found in a great many collections at the present time. When first introduced some of the sleeves were of a soft stretchable plastic which initially tended to hold the slides too firmly, but with use, not firmly enough. Clearly in a busy library this could lead to the frustration of slides falling from the sleeves during retrieval. Questions were also raised concerning the interaction of some types of plastic with the slide emulsion when in such close proximity, and also concerning the possibilities of moisture retention near the slide surface. These early problems have been solved by the use of polypropylene which is a stronger, less pliable plastic and which is of an improved composition for the purpose.

Whereas storage in ring binders is more suitable for smaller-scale collections, storage in filing cabinets is the primary method for storing intermediate to large collections of slides and is especially suitable for collections composed of single images rather than slide sets because of the immediacy and particular suitability for the rapid scanning of many images.

Unclassified arrangement

Although it has been argued that some type of classified arrangement is a first choice for most slide collections, a conscious choice not to adopt a classified arrangement can be a valid course of action according to circumstances. It perhaps needs to be emphasized that the choice does need to be an informed one, since the advantages of a classified order detailed above should not be relinquished without good reason. Quite often collections begin in a very modest way, perhaps in the desk drawer of an individual and large numbers of slides can accumulate without those involved in their management being aware that in due course the stock could form the basis of a fully-fledged slide library. This naturally requires much more attention devoted to its organization and to how the information it contains will be accessed and exploited. By the time large quantities of slides have been collected those involved in the management are usually reluctant to revise the methods which have evolved and which may possibly have become inadequate for a much larger collection. Yet to change to improved methods more appropriate to a sizeable multi-user collection could involve an unacceptably high level of new work. A larger collection is almost certain to have more users with complex and varied needs than did the collection when it was of a more modest size. Furthermore, both a demand for sound organizational methods will be revealed and the shortcomings of inadequacies exposed.

There are, however, a number of good reasons why a classified order for arrangement may not be preferred. These are:

1   If a lack of staff time, expertise or finance is such that the extra work involved in employing a classification cannot be justified. Clearly, it is far easier to mechanically add a slide to a continuous sequence rather than to make a skilful judgement concerning the subject content and the slide's exact placing in a subject arrangement.

2   If the slides are almost invariably required to be retrieved in packages or sequences from storage which have no reference to a subject approach and it is most efficient to store them in a continuous sequential order for this aim to be achieved.

3   Browsing, scanning and image comparison in storage is not judged to be a priority requirement and the retrieval of individual images can be carried out adequately using separately provided indexes.

An unclassified or sequential arrangement can be either by numerical or alphabetical notation.

Numerical arrangement includes accession number order where a consecutive number is affixed to each slide as it is acquired, for example, job number order in, possibly, a building practice, or a number which represents a client in any service situation or a patient in the medical context. Without being explicitly evident a pure accession number or a job number could represent, in effect, a chronological order, without using the date overtly as the filing aspect. In distinction, a number which is representative of a person or other entity may be a compound number (i.e. a series of significant numbers separated by a solidus, colon or hyphen) which places it in a subsequence within the whole collection.

For any collection which includes slides of topical interest and where material diminishes significantly in value to users as time passes, chronological order is appropriate. As files become out of date and less relevant they do not interfere with newly-added, more highly-used images which are meeting current needs. If the collection is constantly renewed and old slides eventually discarded from the collection as a matter of routine then chronological order can further this 'conveyor-belt' process. The date used for chronological order can be either contemporary or historical. The date when the photograph was exposed or processed can be used or the date when the subject of the illustration was created, invented or in the case of people their date of birth.

Alphabetical sequences of arrangement are perhaps the most obvious orderly way in which slides can be arranged. Clearly, people, places, titles of works, etc., can all be accommodated in a straight A–Z sequence without use of controlled headings, lists or the techniques used to make alphabetical arrangements more approachable (or classified as discussed earlier). Usually linear sequences of this type, whether numerical or alphabetical will require further indexes to the other information contained in the collection.

6 Commercially available slide management and retrieval packages

A wide range of computer software is now available for automating either existing slide library procedures or to extend the scope of a collection's retrieval or general management system. At the simplest level packages can be obtained which automate one process or management function. A good example of this is the automated production of slide labels. In this case a microtype printer or one which supports superscript characters can provide compact, clear printing on adhesive labels which enhance the professional appearance of slides, help standardize the information on labels and also make best use of the all too confined area which slide mounts allow for written information. Writing by hand onto slide mounts has always been a tedious and unsatisfactory process leading to inconsistency, possible over-use of abbreviations and eventually erasure due to wear. Although it is possible to automate the labelling operation in isolation it is more usual to make further use of whatever slide data has been stored on computer to also provide some retrieval functions. Budget software packages can, therefore, be purchased which provide these two or further facilities and greatly enhance both the appearance, control and searching of any slide collection.

Naturally many large, busy slide libraries demand more features and are also seeking not only to reproduce and extend what was possible through their former manual systems, but to add powerful stock control and searching facilities. In addition to retrieval and circulation methods it is now a serious option to preserve images electronically for greater security, improved retrieval, and possible editing. At the other end of the scale from the small collection requiring what equates almost to a tidying or streamlining process of laborious and time-consuming manual operations, the large concern may decide to implement a modular system which provides integrated management of images and textual information. This would effectively control cataloguing and circulation together with ordering and acquisition. Indications are that present online public access catalogues (OPACs) in libraries are likely to increasingly incorporate the facilities provided by image databases and that users will have access to on-screen images possibly captured from the parent organization's own picture or slide collection.

In the commercial sphere the routines involved with standard charges, invoicing and accounting are features which require and have received attention and solution. All such features and needs are addressed by a variety of systems produced by the computing industry in what is a growing and competitive market area.

Between the two extremes of automating one library process and of applying a modular system to automate practically all library processes there are a variety of other packages and approaches to automation. The basic approaches to automation are outlined below:

1 Purpose-designed software which automates one management process, e.g. labelling.

2 Use of a general purpose database management system such as dBase IV, Dataease or Paradox. The ability to define the fields required and design a comprehensive in-house system

makes this one of the more flexible options, but naturally staff need the relevant time and expertise to carry out the developmental work, conduct the necessary trials and tailor the basic 'off the shelf' system to the needs of an organization. In larger systems programming expertise may be necessary to extend a system's scope to meet a particular slide library's needs or to integrate other information formats (pictures or text) into the system.

This is a market area where there is the widest range of choice available. Well-established textual databases dominate this market area. Increasingly versions are offered which run under Windows and which incorporate images as an integral feature of database information. Ultimately, flexibility makes this option most attractive. Once a library database has been established, changes to the database design is not a matter to be taken lightly. However, this approach to automation makes adaptation and a greater degree of change a more realistic possibility than do the other options.[1]

3   Use of software written specially by a software company to meet the needs of one type of picture collection.
   e.g.   Commercial picture library.
          Individual freelance photographer.
          Museum.
          Visual arts library.

4   Use of modular systems which integrate library processes as mentioned above with or without an incorporated image database. Such an image database may be designed also to interface with optical disc systems and thus be linked to a wider publishing sector.

In such a new and rapidly developing field and with a survey such as this it is not instructive or equitable to review specific software items and assess their capabilities, strengths and weaknesses. Software producers are constantly endeavouring to improve their products in a market which constantly changes in emphasis. Features which have not previously been included in a package could be offered at quite short notice and it would be unrepresentative to critically condemn a package when most software producers have policies of improvement based on responses to clients' requirements and industry developments.

Currently, there are three client groups for which systems are written and marketed. These are: 1) commercial photographers either individuals or larger concerns; 2) photographic libraries and agencies and 3) academic libraries, museums and archives. It is of value to note that a system designed for a freelance photographer may meet the needs of a small non-commercial slide library or vice-versa. It is, therefore, prudent for prospective buyers to at least examine and preview the features offered by systems which are not necessarily aimed at their sector of the market.

Appendix 3, page 185, provides a current list of a selection of suppliers of automated systems for the management of picture and slide collections.

7 Medical slide collections

The relationship of slide management in the medical field to other fields

The study of slide management and the use of slides in the medical and health care fields is of special interest in information management terms since it provides a clearly-defined subject discipline where slide collections and their use have reached a level of development comparable with that of the visual arts. The academic, visual arts field, however, remains the area where most activity is concentrated and where the most complex challenges regarding indexing and retrieval are to be found.

Whereas the significance and meaning of an image in the fine arts field is often multifaceted, has many references and implications, the images generated by scientific and technical disciplines tend to have a single more direct purpose or subsequent use. Although this is a generalization, the value of a slide, for example, of a particular medical condition is that it has the intention to define that condition and communicate an accurate diagnosis. In rare medical conditions where the visible case symptoms may not be seen for perhaps a considerable time the value of an accurate visual record is obvious for teaching and communication of conditions which students are unlikely to encounter. Of course illustrations of more common conditions and normal anatomy are of equal value for teaching purposes. Thus whereas ambiguity or multiple meanings provide a fascinating enrichment and are an inherent part of the study of the visual arts, any ambiguity is a confusion when dealing with scientific and technological subject-matter and usually needs to be eliminated.[1] It follows from this that indexing the implied meanings in the visual arts field creates complexities of a kind without exact parallel in science and technology.

The development of effective slide management in the medical field has been achieved, as far as can be detected, quite independently and without reference to, or appreciable communication with, slide management activities in other fields. In this connection the medical situation typifies how slide management techniques have evolved in areas other than the visual arts without such ties or communication with other disciplines or organizations. Other technical or scientific areas where slide collections exist are not well documented. Medical record and teaching collections, therefore, by reason of their clear delineation provide something of a case study.

Where professional interest groupings in any slide field are linked strongly by subject interest or other common purpose they are usually either not motivated or have no immediate need to relate to others who are working with slides in other subject areas. However, it is the case that the common medium of the slide format could provide a link between slide managers in differing subject areas if contact was made. In addition to these divisions which exist because of differing subject concerns there is also a sharp difference in connections and outlook between libraries and collections of slides run for commercial reasons and those centred on public or academic services.

As List notes when reviewing *Photo libraries and agencies.* (Askam, 1990)[2]

This reviewer finds it quite remarkable that a work of this sort can be written and published in 1990 without a single mention of Aslib, or the

Library Association, their Audiovisual Groups, ARLIS, the Society of Indexers, the Museum Documentation Association, et al., or various journals on the management of picture collections which emanate from these bodies.

... it rather reinforces the conclusion that as far as a significant portion of the 'visual information profession' is concerned, organisations such as those named above do not exist as worthwhile resources, and that is a rather damning indictment of professional organisations who seek to represent the full spectrum of 'the information profession'.[3]

The book under review comes from the background of the commercial picture supply and is written with photographers, picture researchers, editors and art directors in mind. While praising the thoroughness of the work within its declared limits, List points out that it does not seek to indicate or include as relevant the wider non-commercial picture library world or the appropriate services its representative bodies provide.

Given the present complex and changing state of the organization of picture management in all connections, it is perhaps a harsh judgement to suggest that lack of cross-communication is a particular shortcoming of any corporate body, and much less that of an individual. There are highly-effective groupings working with visual resources of all formats, including slides, which co-ordinate and provide a focus for the contributions of a great many highly-committed individuals making valuable contributions to visual resource management. However, it is true to say that there are several large, but self-contained spheres of interest and activity whose boundaries are rarely crossed either from outside or from within. List expresses some surprise and questions how a book can express such an isolated or specialized position when the more usual appreciation of commercial and academic picture libraries is that they are very wide ranging and varied and outward looking.

One possible reason for a self-contained outlook or approach is that immediate service concerns especially in the commercial sector do not necessitate contact with other libraries which do not contribute to the immediate aim of delivering suitable images to a client. The commercial demands are such that wider theoretical discussion or contact with others is often excluded. The British Association of Picture Libraries (BAPLA), the Society of Picture Researchers and Editors (SPRed), and the various other professional bodies for professional photographers apparently serve well all the essential needs of commercial photographers and others in the commercial picture world and the pressing demands of business and client needs creates a different climate of operation from the academic or non-commercial service sector.

A further possible reason for self-containment, or boundaries between spheres of activity, which applies to all sectors is that slide management is such that the techniques used are tailored to meet local demands and are not thought to be applicable to collections which are dissimilar in aim. Such a view would be a logical deduction from the nature of the reports in the literature from all quarters where many systems have been unique to individual collections. However, though methods may well be unique, if communicated they may possibly trigger applications in other fields, be adapted to others' needs or simply renew the imaginations of those seeking to be creative in their thinking about slide management. The bodies which Link lists in the above quotation as not receiving mention in the reviewed work are unlikely to be seen of immediate value to, for example, the individual freelance photographer or even the picture researcher who are not necessarily image collection *managers*, but are often mainly service *users*.

Furthermore, the managers of many slide collections, and this is particularly true of the medical field, do not operate within, or have close links with, libraries of any kind. Departments of medical illustration hold the overwhelming majority of clinical slides generated in UK hospitals, and their professional body, the Institute of Medical and Biological Illustration (IMBI), does not have an explicit library or information science function although it effectively fulfils a reporting role through its journal,[4] to a necessary extent, when such issues are the concern of its membership. The technical aspects of medical photography *per se* remains the principal focus of IMBI, with collection management a necessary resulting concern brought about by the accumulation of images by individual clinicians, photographers and departments of medical illustration within hospitals. Medical libraries do not figure prominently in holding large slide stocks in the UK nor are there formal links between medical libraries and departments of medical illustration. A number of medical libraries hold modest quantities of slide sets or tape/slide sequences, and with only a few exceptions do not stock collections designed or composed to retrieve individual images.

The point here, however, is that any advance in, or discussion of, image or slide collection management in a field such as medicine is not immediately, or in the medium-term, going to be seen as relevant, much less be communicated to someone working in a fine arts library, a picture agency or elsewhere. Moreover, the medical field has effectively been a leader in capturing or transferring still images to analogue videodisc and this experience is invaluable in evaluating and assessing the importance and usefulness of the many microcomputer and CD developments which are emerging at present in other areas of image storage and use. Although there have been a number of videodisc compilations in medicine, both interactive and non interactive, the *UK National Medical Slide Bank* on videodisc compiled by Graves Educational Resources and published jointly with Chadwyck-Healey is one of the most significant developments in slide management. Although there are at present a number of initiatives using CD-ROM technologies to capture images in the visual arts and other fields there appear to be few examples of analogue videodisc being exploited in quite the same directly successful way as the Graves project. However, the high profile of this technology in both analogue and digital form is more than likely to play a growing role in picture handling in all fields.

It is creditable that there is a discernable willingness within the visual arts field to include slide collections from other fields in research efforts and data gathering, but there are few tangible results of this desire. Such an outward-looking disposition is not evident when other areas in which slides are employed are considered. The academic picture and slide world of the visual arts appears to be more aware of reaching out to others managing pictures in other connections. However, it is evident that there are a variety of viewpoints.

I have always found art librarianship fascinating, partly because art librarians refuse to join much of the professional stampede towards the information society. They deal with materials which, while they do not bypass other librarians, are usually of secondary interest to them – the visual image rather than the printed page; artefacts and realia rather than texts; items which often lack neat descriptors like authors, titles and publishers.[5]

There is an unconscious and tacit assumption in much that is written in the visual arts field that the terms visual image and visual resource equals a visual relating to art history, the fine arts or possibly museums and art galleries, but not to any other discipline or field. However, there are close equivalents outside the visual arts areas regarding some of the problems which arise. For example, pathological specimens in medicine present similar problems as do artefact and realia in the art world and slide images of the same specimens present similar problems to cataloguers and indexers by virtue of format as well as subject considerations.

Anomalies such as the absence of title pages are well known to audio-visual librarianship irrespective of subject field and are approached initially with format considerations taking precedence over subject concerns. From the point of view of the theoretical and practical information professional it is the common format which is as important as the subject matter of a collection and it follows from this that the techniques pioneered in quite dramatically different subject and service contexts can have valuable lessons and find application in quite disparate subject areas or information management situations. Whether the scope of a slide collection is international, national or regional or its coverage broad or specialized, whether its clientele are in the public or private sphere or whether the information function is archival or current, educational, leisure or research-based the common factor of the slide format should provide a contact point for those involved in slide library management. Naturally, differences and necessary refinements will continue to exist, but some common base should be possible.

Perhaps, because of being the first in the field with regard to many developed techniques of picture management, the visual arts area has tended to claim for its own terminology that which would normally be regarded of universal applicability. The traditional curricular or academic divide between the arts and sciences is possibly another factor in the lack of exchange between those working with slides in the differing areas. This and the commercial or non-commercial purposes are perhaps the two strongest negative influences creating obstacles to a more free exchange of slide management information between interested parties. Such difficulties are part of cultural, social and professional developments rather than a deliberate creation or neglect by any corporate body or the over-assertiveness or apathy of individuals. It is within this overall context and set of relationships or their absence that slide utilization in the medical field is set. It is likely that the medical field about which a moderate amount of information exists typifies very broadly the situation in other scientific and technical fields where slides are used, but about which there is little substantial data. Further statements concerning scientific or technical slide collections would be speculative.

Medical slide collections in the UK

Since the very earliest days of photography it was clear that the invention would have great application in recording routine scientific and technical work of all kinds, and innovation and its attendant processes. Medical science was not slow to take up the use of photography for recording patient conditions and documenting either the progress of disease or the beneficial effects of treatment. The value of the objective recording of the visible effects of rare conditions which could only previously be conveyed by written or verbal description or hand drawings was of great importance to medical education and its progress. By late Victorian times, as Williams notes, medical photography already included examples of pathology specimens and the use of photomicrography techniques.[6] Naturally black-and-white print material was used, but the lantern slide found favour for medical lectures to sizeable audiences.

Modern collections of 35mm medical slides are generally to be found in departments of medical illustration or medical photography within hospitals or medical schools and are used for medical teaching, recording patient conditions and for supplying illustrative material for republication in journals. This combination of functions – academic/educational, research, administrative and publication – places real and potential demands on medical slide collections which are perhaps unique in this respect among all types of slide collections. Usually slide collections in other areas fulfil only one or perhaps two of the above functions.

It is estimated that there are upwards of 5–6 million slides in medical establishments in Great Britain. The generally rapid rate at which slides in all fields are produced makes any precise figure impossible, and the continued expansion of existing collections is always highly likely. Although the earliest collections of 35mm colour slides in medical institutions began almost as soon as the format and processes became generally available in the 1930s it was not until the post-war years of developing prosperity in the 1950s and 1960s that rapid expansion took place resulting in sizeable collections. Such developments were centred on the large, prestigious teaching hospitals where a high demand for quality illustrative matter for lectures was generated as it continues to be today. It is reasonable to assume, though it can not be substantiated here, that large or intermediate-sized regional hospitals were also creating slides whether or not they went on to develop structured collections of the images generated. No uniform pattern, however, emerges with regard to the size of collections. A large present-day medical slide collection in a university teaching hospital would number between 80,000 and 120,000 slides, but a more average size would be in the region of 30,000 to 50,000 slides.

The advances both in medical science and photographic technology have led to slide images being made of internal parts of the body both by X-ray and invasive techniques such as fibre optics. The wider application of photography in this way to record images other than purely externally visible surface features has led over the years to more images being generated and thus entering slide storage systems. Although straight comparisons of the total numbers of slides held are not intrinsically vitally important facts, and there is no comprehensive or conclusive quantitative data available, the medical field is second only as an academic discipline to the visual arts as a collector/user of slide resources in a controlled manner. The upper limit for visual arts collections appears to be in the region of 500,000 and such figures are only exceeded by the larger slide collections in the commercial and publishing world or by the few collections of national importance.

Unlike slides generated in other subject areas the slides acquired in departments of medical illustration are almost all created within the respective departments and few are purchased, donated or acquired by exchange agreements, although a minority of slides find their way into collections via these methods. Collections now also have the choice of supplementing their collections by the purchase of images from Graves Educational Resources *UK National Medical Slide Bank* or obtaining the compilation of 12,440 definitive images from Graves on videodisc. The comprehensively assembled and packaged 'Slide Atlases' from Wolfe also provide an excellent quality service. However, it is not the case that all departments of medical illustration retain the slides they create in-house or have responsibility for images or photographic records after the technical photographic processes have been completed. A wide variety of local arrangements exist between individual clinicians, medical staff and other specialist departments of hospitals. Very rarely are slides forwarded to medical libraries for subsequent cataloguing or loan. This may be a disappointment to some information professionals, but could also be greeted with immense relief by others who are aware of the labour intensive, often detailed and painstaking work necessary to either establish a working collection of unitary slide images or adapt an existing one to meet client needs.

On occasion, departments of medical illustration do not hold slides for one or more positive reasons. These are usually based on their perceived or defined role and service responsibilities within a particular hospital. Some departments of medical illustration, for example, see their function as being purely confined to creating photographic images and delivering them to the user who then has the responsibility for their use and all subsequent care of the images. Others make the judgement that the slides are only of interest to the requesting clinician and, therefore, such images would find no wider use even if slide collections were built up. This, combined with the fact that some consultants actively wish to collect and hold personal collections covering their specialist interests, ensures that many smaller-scale slide collections are often held at various locations within hospitals and medical schools. Added to this, and to further complicate the overall situation, is that particular departments have a special preference for slides in the course of their work. Pathology laboratories figure prominently in this connection and sizeable collections devoted solely to pathology are not uncommon. Orthopaedics, dermatology and X-ray departments also appear to the fore in having an interest in slide-accumulation within their respective departments.

In many instances, therefore, it would be wrong to assume that departments of medical illustration have a monopoly of slide holdings or that they necessarily hold the majority of slides for any particular institution. The total holdings of other specialist departments could in some cases well exceed the number held centrally by the department of medical illustration. It is sometimes the case that multiple copies of slides are made. The most likely destinations for these are patient records, the requesting individual and the centralized collection in the department of medical illustration. In summary the state of slides in hospitals is well described by Hedley and Morton.

It is one of the main functions of every medical illustration or photographic department to deal with routine requests for clinical photographs of patients, and teaching hospitals in the UK must be producing something in the region of 600,000 clinical colour transparencies in a five year period. If large district general hospitals and other institutions are also taken into account this figure may well be over 1 million. It is not clear what actually happens to most of this material: there may even be dispute as to ownership: much of it is uncatalogued and cloistered in desks, drawers and cabinets, and available for teaching only at the individual clinician's discretion.[7]

Although this was written in 1976 it appears that no substantial change has taken place since that time. Whereas the adoption of automated management and retrieval methods have improved access to existing centralized collections of slides, it is not clear if there has been a more purposeful trend towards channelling the many slides created in hospitals into structured collections where they will be held in common, have their existence publicized and their use made more freely available. The extent to which medical libraries could assist to further this process may appear clear to many information professions, but has not been adopted on any appreciable scale. Since medical libraries have existing links with many different user groups they are ideally placed to reach potential slide user groups not as well served as consultants. Such personnel are medical students, nursing staff, paramedical staff, general practitioners and health visitors, dentists, radiologists and physiotherapists either within the confines of the parent medical institution or a wider administrative area.

The issue of confidentiality of patient records
Although opposition to centralized collections of slides is not common in the medical sphere such attitudes do exist. All medical records involving patient identities and including photographic images necessarily involve the issue of confidentiality and patient confidence in the integrity of the patient–doctor relationship. Although reluctance to maintain centralized collections of slides cannot be attributed directly to a desire to avoid the difficulties associated with the confidentiality of patient records, the issue does provide a constant consideration which has to be addressed by hospital authorities. The issue can be a contributory reason, along with others, for a medical slide collection not being held. It is standard practice to obtain the patient's consent for photographs to be taken and for them to be subse-

quently used to further treatment or teaching, in the closely controlled hospital environment and in a professional and responsible manner. When republication of images is a consideration then it has to be ensured that the identity of the patient is obscured. It is not unknown for litigation to result following a discovery of a breach of this undertaking and thus confidentiality is rightly taken very seriously. The very seriousness with which the matter is viewed is perhaps another reason why collections in some hospitals are under the custodial care of individual specialists where a closer control can be maintained over confidentiality and case histories.

It is usually a practical proposition for centralized collections of slides to be successfully held and exploited without contravening confidentiality agreements, but in library terms this can remain a constant obstacle to the widespread exchange, distribution, republication, or informal general use of slide holdings. It is perhaps partly because of this that there has been an understandable reluctance for departments of medical illustration to relinquish direct control of their slides by passing them to medical libraries for instance, since photographers have undertaken the personal obligation to preserve confidentiality. In the library situation the issue of confidentiality can come into greater conflict with the general policy or *raison d'etre* of libraries to make their stocks as freely available as possible within their declared user group. While confidentiality is an ever present consideration and a professional anxiety to people of conscience, it has been shown that it can be respected without restricting the use of slides to the point where access is almost completely closed and effective use stifled. Table 3 broadly summarizes, therefore, the possible locations of slides in large hospitals and the likely users when slides are held in these particular locations.

Retrieval of medical slides

Classification and other schemes applicable to medical slide collections
A wider variety of available classification schedules, controlled lists of terms, thesauri or authority files and numerical represen-

Location	Usual users
Collections held by individual consultants.	Often only the consultant. Loans at the discretion of the clinician.
Patient records departments.	Do not always hold slides, but when held they are well documented when stored with medical notes. Clearly, use limited to purely a record role.
Specialist medical departments, e.g. pathology.	Hold slides relevant to their specialized work. No obligation, need or motivation to necessarily make slides available to other parties.
Departments of medical illustration.	Hold the largest centralized slide collections, which have widest range of users within hospitals, but do not necessarily reach all groups who could use slides.
Medical libraries.	With a few exceptions do not hold large numbers of slides, but are in the best position and have the greatest potential for exploiting slides by making them more widely available to known and new user groups.

Table 3 Possible location of slides in hospitals and their likely users

tations of subjects than would possibly be first assumed, is appropriate for adoption or adaptation to the classification of medical slides. Although there appears to be no report of Simons and Tansey's classification scheme being used with medical slides, the preface of the scheme is worth consulting for its analysis of general principles.[8] None of the other schemes below, however, were designed for use with illustrations, but that is not necessarily a drawback in assessing their suitability. A number of the specialized schemes do provide comprehensive coverage of the medical science field and it is from this list that slide managers in this subject area are most likely to find a method by which to arrange their slide stocks.

Strohlein provides a more thorough coverage and evaluation of the various options.[9] Although Strohlein includes throughout his work considerations concerning automated retrieval, developments in this area have been such that this aspect of his work is now dated. The 80-column card format for computer input to which Strohlein refers is no longer a limitation on input. Both Cilliers[10] and Barker and Harden[11] also make valuable contributions in comparing the relative specificity of various schemes. The manual use of post co-ordinate indexing systems discussed by Strohlein, Barker and Harden and by Hedley and Morton[12] are now effectively obsolete for sizeable, developed collections since modern microcomputers and database systems fulfil this function with greater efficiency.[13] Study of these contributions is of value for understanding what is required and for conceptualizing some of the operations and functions carried out by the computer. Whereas it was usual when using a manual system to either arrange slides in an appropriate classified order with separate card file indexes or arrange them in accession number order with a post co-ordinate system it is now possible to combine the best aspects of these two options by maintaining a classified order and co-ordinating subjects at the search stage of an enquiry, by key-word enquiries, provided by automated indexing methods.

The origins and original purposes of the schemes and lists available can either make them attractive or inappropriate options for any given slide collection. None can be said to have general overriding advantages over the others and much less be said to provide an ideal arrangement order.

The main criteria by which the slide manager must judge these classifications and terminology lists, with automation as a background consideration, are principally as follows.

1   Specificity: does the scheme specify specialist subjects accurately or is it so general that too many slides will have the same subject number?

2   Does the scope of the scheme broadly coincide with that of the collection?

3   If the scope of the collection expands or changes will the scheme cater for this?

4   Does the scheme have revised editions which keep pace with changing medical knowledge?

5   Length of numbers (are they simply too long to be written on slide mounts or too cumbersome to follow)?

6   If an automated system is to be used does it allow for the entry of the classification scheme's notation? Are the field lengths provided adequate? Are they fixed or changeable.

7   Is the notation of a simple alphabetical or numerical order (citation order) or not?

8   Does the scheme bring together subjects in a way which is appropriate for the collection?

9   Would it be more appropriate to store the slides in patient, project, lecture or simply chronological order or can such approaches be incorporated more conveniently within a database? Who uses the collection and for what purposes will largely determine the answer to this question.

10   Are alphabetical subject headings a realistic option?

General Book Classifications

Faceted schemes   Such schemes specify concepts only, which are then combined by the classifier in a precisely prescribed way to specify complex subjects, e.g. *Colon classification* (Ranganathan, 1971).

Enumerative schemes   These set out to specify a number for every subject or concept. (see Chapter 5).

Although general classifications which cover the whole of knowledge do not usually provide the detail necessary for specialized medical collections they should not be summarily dismissed for this reason. They can be of value under certain circumstances. A number of general health care and biomedical slide collections, for example, hold images which are not inherently medical, but relate to the workings of a particular institution. Images such as personnel, hospital buildings and equipment or health and safety may require separate classification. General classifications may well be applicable to such material.

The Universal Decimal Classification (UDC) (British Standards Institution) is of special note in this respect since it has both general and subject specific schedules. Similarly, the medical classification section which appears in the *Library of Congress Classification (LCC)* was used as the basis for the *National Library of Medicine Classification (NLM)*. Furthermore, local extensions to the existing specified numbers in book schemes could yield the necessary detail to define subjects of slides in some collections, e.g. *Bliss Bibliographic Classification; Dewey Decimal Classification; Library of Congress Classification; Universal Decimal Classification (General Scheme)* (BSI).

Medical Book Classifications
National Library of Medicine Classification (NLM); Cunningham's Classification for Medical Literature; Universal Decimal Classification (Medical schedules) (BSI).

The NLM scheme is now the established standard classification for use in medical libraries and its familiarity in this context is a distinct advantage in its use with slides in medical connections.

Systems used by periodical indexing/abstracting services

Medical Subject Headings (MeSH); NLM; Excerpta Medica. These systems of headings stem from the need to index the vast periodical literature generated by biomedical activity across the world. Medical Subject Headings (MeSH) is the thesaurus of *Index Medicus*, the primary indexing service of biomedical periodical literature and is published annually by the National Library of Medicine (NLM).

The National Library of Medicine has the impressive status of being the world's largest research library in a single scientific and professional field and numbers some five million items including pictorial material. Over 3,000 periodical titles are indexed. The on-line version of *Index Medicus* is called MEDLINE and currently contains seven million references. As can be imagined, data handling of such a magnitude and the indexing of such vast resources results in almost exhaustive subject indexing.

As in so many other areas CD-ROM versions of bibliographic and other databases are becoming increasingly popular and are likely to dominate if not supersede their on-line parents. The future of microfiche in these areas can now only be very limited mainly due to its inability to compete with the automated indexing provided by on-line and CD-ROM versions. Although there are a number of CD-ROM versions of MEDLINE the services of both *DIALOG OnDisc – Medline* and *MEDLINE on SilverPlatter* include the full MeSH listing with indexes. The SilverPlatter version covers the entire database since its inception in 1966 in several volumes (each volume consisting of a number of discs). The current volume dates from 1988 and is updated monthly. In comparison the Dialog version covers only the last six years of MEDLINE and is updated quarterly. In such a rapidly changing field both with respect to medical information and the storage/retrieval technology other services can grow quickly to compete with those which are established and current sources of CD-ROMs available need to be constantly checked.

Returning to MeSH as directly applied to slides, however, it is more than capable of meeting the subject coverage needs of almost any medical slide collection. Another possible advantage is that MeSH is constantly updated to keep pace with medical knowledge. Although this feature ensures that a subject number can almost always be found to allocate to a new slide it can have the drawback of requiring extensive changes to existing numbers for items already processed in a slide collection and such alterations to systems can prove a two-edged sword. The length of the notational numbers created by MeSH is also a matter where slide managers need to strike a compromise between the degree of specificity and the practical considerations of comprehension, convenience and physical space on slide mounts or field lengths in a database system. Other pitfalls can be variations in British and American usage and the problems common to all alphabetical subject headings lists (see Chapter 5). These are use of synonyms and preferred terms and consistency in the use of inversion of compound terms. Help, however, is at hand since an accompanying key-word index is available for the A–Z list of MeSH terms. MeSH is structured in a 'tree' formation leading from general to specific subjects (a hierarchical structure). This provides a logical physical juxtaposition of slides in storage and facilitates browsing and the convenient comparison of like images. On balance and with these provisos MeSH remains a popular and sound choice for arranging and providing subject access to medical slide collections.

Although the *Excerpta Medica* classification and its accompanying Master List of Medical Indexing Terms should be checked for appropriateness for medical slide classification it is unlikely to offer the comprehensive coverage of MeSH or its detailed specificity.

Medical classifications
International Classification of Diseases (ICD) 9th ed., World Health Organization.

One of the most appropriate and widely-used classifications used to classify slide collections, ICD was designed as a classification of diseases, injuries and causes of death. It has been used to code and tabulate mortality and morbidity statistics and to code hospital and other medical records for purposes of storage and retrieval. Such subject coverage as ICD provides corresponds more closely to the usual content of medical slide collections than do the more general classifications such as the NLM scheme. The further facts that the scheme had its origin in the World Health Organization of the United Nations is a reliable guarantee of a secure future and continuing revisions. It is a commendation of the system that it was adopted by the *UK National Medical Slide Bank* for the arrangement of the images on its videodisc.

Other medical classifications of note

The following classifications are mentioned in the literature and although possibly only of use in a small minority of specialized collections are worthy of note: *Hull Disease Coding*, Dr F.M. Hull (adaptation of ICD); *Current Medical Information and Terminology (CMIT)*; American Medical Association; *International Histological Classification of Tumours*; World Health Organization of the United Nations.

Specialized vocabularies/ thesauri/authority files

Likewise the following vocabularies could be of value to specialized collections: *Standard Nomenclature of Diseases and Operations*, American Medical Association, 5th ed, 1961; *Systematized Nomenclature of Pathology (SNOP)*, College of American Pathologists; *Systematized Nomenclature of Medicine (SNOMed)*, College of American Pathologists.

8 Optical disc systems and the slide

Introduction

This chapter provides details of optical disc systems which include the storage of still images among their capabilities and are thus likely to increasingly affect the future of the slide. It covers the major features of the analogue and digital disc systems and the rival developments competing for similar places in the market. Only time will reveal exactly where the new systems will either replace or work in conjunction with existing slide collections. Naturally, of the many systems being developed some have far greater relevance to the issue of the storage of still images than others and, therefore, for present purposes require closer attention. It is necessary to mention briefly some formats, for example the audio compact disc (CD-DA), which though they have no application for illustrative matter are at the base of the technological developments relating to CD systems and are part of the same technology. This leads onto the image-storing disc systems such as Photo-CD which have a closer relationship with existing photographic images.

Although the main strands and direction of developments are discernable, work remains to be done both technically, but also psychologically to convince customers, particularly in the domestic sector, that they need the multimedia technology which is becoming available. As this is achieved it is probable that the present number of systems could be reduced or merged to result in a few commercial winners. It is success in continental or worldwide domestic markets which reduces unit costs and leads to the proliferation of a technology, and it is this aspect of the new image-creating media which has to come about before systems become generally in evidence in homes, educational establishments, libraries and elsewhere. The phenomenal market success of the audio compact disc and the video cassette recorder illustrates what can take place and how costs can fall. It also has to be noted that in such a rapidly advancing field the specifications and achievements expressed here represent minimums. The pace of progress in the field invariably exceeds the speed at which events can be reported.

The effects of technological advancement

It is now generally appreciated how word-processing systems have transformed the control which can be exercised over the creation, amendment and rearrangement of bodies of text, ranging from the briefest of office memos to multi-volume scholarly works. Also textual databases, hypertext and free text searching have led to new levels of access to the content of electronically-stored literature. Such advancements have found application in all areas where words are employed, from basic office administration in small businesses to multinational publishing corporations and media concerns.

A similar transformation brought about by the increasing power of computers is now taking place involving the machine's ability to store, process and create or reproduce pictorial information. Many technical difficulties exist concerned with the automated storage and display of illustrations in comparison with textual matter. One of the fundamental limitations of earlier

microcomputers was their lack of storage capacity and processing power to hold, display or manipulate images. In order to
appreciate the much greater storage needed to effectively record
images of acceptable definition it is necessary to begin with the
basic units of computer storage and make some comparisons.

Image data storage
The electronics of the computer recognizes the binary digits 0 or
1. Eight such digits or bits form one byte which normally represents one character, the fundamental computing unit. These and
the higher order units are as follows:

8 binary digits (bits)	=	1 byte (character)
1,024 bytes	=	1 kilobyte (kb)
1,048,576 bytes	=	1 megabyte (mb)
1,073,741,824 bytes	=	1 gigabyte (gb)

Often in everyday usage these precise figures are rounded for
convenience as follows:

1,000 bytes	=	1 kb
1,000 kb	=	1 mb
1,000 mb	=	1 gb

If we consider that one full page of A4 text can take up to 2.5kb of
storage and that a CD-ROM disc has a capacity of 650mb it follows that the disc can hold 250,000 sides of A4 text. This represents 100 million words or for those wishing to preserve their
shelf space and everyone's forests, 2,835 lbs of paper! These
impressive figures, which apply to text storage are put in another
perspective, however, when digitally-stored images are considered.

A 35mm slide of standard resolution (100 ISO) requires 10mb
of storage and high-quality resolution can increase this figure up
to 18mb. Using the lower value it can be seen that a slide requires
4,000 times more storage capacity than a page of A4 text. The
650mb CD-ROM could, therefore, in theory hold only 65 slides
and the standard PC hard disc (e.g. 180mb) and present floppy

discs (1.4mb) provide no option for slide or picture storage. Although data compression techniques have been developed which economize on the storage capacity needed to hold images this has reduced and managed the problem rather than eliminated the difficulties of storing images digitally. If a much reduced quality illustration is acceptable then illustrations can be incorporated effectively in textual information as has been achieved with CD-ROM versions of newspapers and encyclopedias etc.

Motion pictures

Although the still image in the form of the 35mm slide is the concern here, it is also of value to be aware of motion picture developments since multimedia systems are striving to achieve full-screen, full-motion video. The illusion of movement is always created from rapidly displayed still images whether cine film, television or video is used to transmit the pictures. Acceptable flicker-free motion demands 24–30 frames/second to be received by the human observer. Cine film motion uses 24 frames/sec. and standard video reproduction as used in the UK and Europe 25 frames/sec. Not only do present hard discs and CD-ROM's lack sufficient storage space (1 CD-ROM could store less than half a minute of full-screen, full-motion video at present), but the data transfer rates of the devices are too slow to replay the information at the required rate.

In simple terms the compression of data involves analysis of an image and the storage only of sufficient data to reproduce the original to the required standard. If, for example, an image of a landscape is made up in large part of an expanse of similarly coloured blue sky this can be stored much more economically than a detailed foreground, a complex work of art or a human face. When the image is displayed and the data retrieved and decompressed, interpolations are made between the stored picture elements to recreate an image of predetermined resolution. Although there are even more complexities involved with image enhancement or editing, it is at this stage that what is considered acceptable definition becomes crucial. Clientele naturally have varying requirements where faithful reproduction and picture definition are concerned. The art historian and the medical consultant possibly have a higher-standard requirement than the advertising or travel agency.

Compression ratios of 1:100 and 1:160 have been achieved leading to several thousand still images or a number of hours of video being stored on a CD-ROM. All the foregoing refers to image data which is reduced to 0s and 1s and recorded in this form – digitally – for computer storage, processing and retrieval. Before progressing to review a number of the developing systems which exploit this digital-based technology it is important to understand how analogue videodisc differs from its digital cousins and what advantages and disadvantages this represents for the user.

Digital and analogue systems – basic comparison

An analogue device (such as a conventional clock dial) provides a continuous representational reading of a variable message. By contrast a digital device (such as a digital watch) takes and records readings or valuations at discrete intervals. All optical discs employ a tightly-focused laser beam to scan the disc surface. However, whereas with the digital disc the laser reads patterns of 0s and 1s for the computer's interpretation, in the case of the analogue device the laser reads and transmits a constant video signal directly to the video monitor. Since analogue videodisc does not involve computer processing of the image the quality of the image is determined at the input or capture stage by the camera and by the technical quality of the playback equipment. Thus, whereas an analogue signal can be degraded during creation and transmission the quality of a digital image is completely preserved through the integrity of the 0s and 1s recorded pattern. This quality leads to digital systems being referred to as 'no loss' systems by some of the literature. However, at present analogue videodisc has a greater capacity for still images with 54,000 good television standard still-images per side of a 12-inch disc.

As Clark[1] makes clear, an erroneous assumption has grown up that digital technology is inherently more advanced and superior to analogue for every application. This is possibly a result of the dramatic way in which the popular compact, digitally-mastered audio disc superseded analogue recordings on vinyl LP discs in recent years. Since gramophone recordings were notorious for static noise, scratching of the vinyl surface and ultimately subject to wear, the noise-free recordings of the CD were instantly and quite rightly accepted by all except the nostalgic as a superior product. However, this does not hold true for all cases where analogue and digital systems offer apparently similar ways of storing and retrieving data. The true position is that an informed choice needs to be made between the differing systems based on the requirements of a project and the end users. In basic terms and with the present state of development of the technology, analogue disc systems provide the better method of randomly accessing large numbers of still pictures. If the user wishes to use images in conjunction with text, sound and computer graphics or edit an image then digital systems are becoming the preferred alternative. As will be described later sound and text can also be contained on analogue videodisc and used interactively. Clearly, successful systems have been developed using both technologies and it would be a rash prediction to suggest that one method could supersede the other or render it obsolete.

Read Only (RO), Write Once, Read Many (WORM), Write Many Read Many (WMRM) and Direct Read After Write (DRAW)

Another fundamental aspect of electronic data storage both analogue or digital is the ability of a medium to be used repeatedly to store data which can be erased and written over. The value of such devices to the user is already well established. Examples which already exist are videotape (analogue) and computer hard and floppy discs (digital). The ability of a device to do this makes it much more flexible, though less secure, and in the case of optical disc more technically difficult to develop.

The three categories of device which exist are Read Only (RO), Write Once, Read Many times (WORM) and Write Many, Read Many times (WMRM).

RO devices

Data is, in effect, sealed into the device at the manufacturing stage and cannot be subsequently amended or deleted, only replayed. This is true of the compact audio disc and CD-ROM, for example (see table below).

WORM devices

Data can be added on a number of separate occasions to the medium, but cannot be subsequently amended or deleted. Examples of WORM devices are Photo-CD and CRVdisc.

Another acronym used as an alternative to describe the same qualities as WORM is DRAW – Direct Read After Write (see table below).

WMRM devices

Data can be written and erased repeatedly (not included in table below).

Existing computer-backing store peripherals hard and floppy disc already perform this function as does digital audio tape (DAT).

The newer devices in this category are CD-MO (Compact Disc Magneto Optical) a combination of magnetic and optical technology which provides much greater capacity than existing devices for digital storage. The greater access speeds and capacities of the newer media are required for the successful development of high-definition, digitally-stored image databases where there is a prerequisite for massive and fast-backing store. Research is at its most intense in perfecting these devices.

The development of optical disc systems
Table 4 categorizes the main RO and WORM optical disc systems both analogue and digital.

Appendix 1, page 181 should be referred to here for interpretation of the many acronyms and abbreviations used in this table.

OPTICAL DISC

ANALOGUE (Videodisc)		DIGITAL (Compact Disc)		
RO	WORM	RO	RO (PC based)	WORM
Philips 'LaserVision' Pioneer 'LaserDisc'	Sony CRV disc	CD-DA CD-V	CD-ROM CD+G	Kodak/ Philips Photo-CD and Portfolio -CD
Linear and Advanced Interactive Videodisc (AIV)	Panasonic Optical Memory disc recorder (OMDR)	Philips CD-I	Sony CD-ROM XA	
	Optical Disc Corporation Recordable Laser Video- disc (RLV)	Commodore CDTV	Intel/ Microsoft and others DVI	

Table 4   Optical disc systems

Analogue videodisc (Read Only Systems)
The literature variously refers to videodisc as laser disc, laser videodisc, laser vision disc or LV disc. Although 20cm discs are available the 30cm disc is the more common, resembling the 12-inch vinyl LP in size, but not appearance, since videodisc has a silver surface exactly like CDs. 'LaserVision' is the trade name of the Philips system and 'LaserDisc' that of the system developed by Pioneer. All analogue videodisc requires and uses is a dedi-

cated player, that is a player specifically designed to play only analogue videodisc. There are two modes of operation – Constant Linear Velocity (CLV) and Constant Angular Velocity (CAV) and players can operate in either mode. The laser is analogous to the record stylus reading continuously and lineally the profile of the disc to reproduce the audio or video signals. Unlike the record stylus the laser starts its travel from the middle of the disc and progresses outward when playing sequences; for random access of still images it moves rapidly to predetermined locations on the disc surface. One track carries video signals and there are two audio tracks which can be used together for stereo sound or independently for separate sound tracks. CLV mode is non-interactive and is employed to relay up to one hour per side of full motion video. CLV mode is, therefore, a competitor of video-tape offering a more durable copy of feature films, for example, but without the reusable flexibility of videotape and is not the mode used for still picture storage.

In CAV mode videodisc can store 54,000 still images of good television quality on each side of a 30cm disc. This vast volume of storage can be used up entirely of course to provide 108,000 images, but it is more usually the case that many projects dealing with still images do not require the full capacity to fulfil their purposes. If this is the case it is possible to cater for two different television standards on either side of the disc. Furthermore, each frame on a videodisc can be individually located by its own unique address and retrieved in under two seconds. This capacity of storage and retrieval time remain unique qualities of analogue videodisc which have not as yet been equalled by digital systems. Also since analogue videodisc has been available since the late 1970's a number of control software packages have been developed and established prior to the rapid developments in microcomputer and latterly CDs in the mid- to late 1980s. Analogue videodisc has remained, however, essentially a professionally-based and utilized product rather than a success on the domestic market. As a consequence, costs have remained relatively high. It can be seen that there is a direct application of analogue videodisc to the area of service provided at present by collections of still images in print or slide format. Videodisc projects involving the compilations of choice images have drawn on the resources of established slide libraries and indeed have been used to:

1　Increase awareness and use of existing slide collections.
2　Increase sales of conventionally-produced photographic slides.
3　Create more interest in the subject material, and generation of new images thereby strengthening the base of resources available.
4　Provide definitive eclectic sets of top quality images covering specific academic or practical fields of interest.

The complementary development of technology such as this in conjunction with established formats such as the slide is perhaps a more likely way in which events will unfold in the future than the more dramatic prediction that one technology will totally supersede and replace another. This is not to say that the latter does or cannot take place, but it is possibly more attractive for commentators to forecast complete replacement rather than a co-operative and beneficial coexistence and interplay of the new and not so new technologies.

Four different levels of sophistication are available from video-disc equipment.

Level 0　This simply provides linear playback with the most basic of control.
Level 1　A key pad gives stop and search functions. Still image databases can be effectively searched at this level, but only by their predetermined address number entered via the key pad.
Level 2　The computer control track either in key pad or on one of the disc's tracks provides programmed control.
Level 3　The disc player is interfaced with an external computer for more complex use. This can be full interactive pro-grammes, but for still image purposes and of relevance to slides, subject and other retrieval software can be added to create multi access entry points to the images.

Specific projects began as soon as the technology became available and many have been updated as the systems surrounding analogue videodisc have developed. The BBC Doomsday Discs utilized an Archimedes computer to give access and control to geographical, historical and social information supplied by schools and other contributors. Contributors submitted slides and prints as the basic photographic images or raw material which was then scanned or captured onto the videodisc. Other major projects exploiting the technology are the Graves *UK National Medical Slide Bank on Videodisc* and in the fine arts field the National Gallery of Art Disc (Washington DC) to name only two.

Although the 30cm disc remains the more familiar size of videodisc and the current leader for still image storage capacity (54,000 images per side), the smaller size of 20cm (25,200 images per side) is obtainable.

Analogue Videodisc (Write Once Read Many systems)
The more recently developed Sony CRVdisc (CRV = Component Recording Video), Panasonic Optical Memory Disc Recorder (OMDR) and the Optical Disc Corporation's Recordable Laser Videodisc (RLV) enable the user to create programmes or image banks in-house by recording material onto videodisc for immediate playback. These systems are not compatible with the RO LaserVision and LaserDisc systems described above.

Although expensive, such systems have great potential for slide and picture libraries wishing to transfer slide collections to the more durable videodisc format. At present the Sony CRVdisc can hold 36,250 frames per side making it a competitive option in technical terms.

Digital Compact Disc (Read Only systems)

Non-PC-based systems   Two varieties of CD which though they have no still picture relevance need passing mention if only for the purposes of elimination and clarification. These are the most familiar CD format the audio compact disc or CD-DA (Compact Disc Digital Audio) and the less familiar CD-V (Compact Disc Video). CD-V is distinguished by its gold colour and is designed to carry continuous play video and audio and is, therefore, a competitor of the analogue videodisc (CLV) and conventional video tape. CD-V is a hybrid format in the sense that the audio is carried digitally and the video in analogue form.

Of greater interest in this section of CD formats, however, are the Philips and Commodore rival multimedia systems about which much has been promised. The Philips development is called CD-I (Compact Disc-Interactive) and the Commodore version is known as CDTV (Commodore Dynamic Total Vision). Although one of the main concerns of the research and development is to provide full-screen, full-motion video pictures as an integral part of the packages, the potential for still picture/slide image storage is also appreciable. The systems are aimed at the educational/domestic market.

CD-I requires a specialized, dedicated player which interfaces with the domestic TV set and hi-fi system. An added bonus of the system is that it not only plays audio CD, but also the Philips electronic photograph disc storage system Photo-CD (see below). Using a compression ratio of 1:100 it has been claimed that the system will store 13,000 still pictures. The announcement of a disc of still images entitled 'Renaissance Gallery' heralds an application of CD-I technology to an area hitherto reserved for slides. The involvement of both Sony and Matsushita in agreeing worldwide standards seems to ensure a firm future for CD-I, but its full acceptance and establishment has yet to become a reality. CDTV is intended to provide similar multimedia programmes based on the use of the Amiga computer games microcomputer and a standard CD-ROM drive. Both CD-I and CDTV are, however, based on an 8-bit standard and some commentators believe this will prove a limitation in the long term and lead to the systems eventually being overhauled by the next generation of systems based on 32-bit technology. Matsushita and Time-Warner are currently developing 3DO, a 32 bit system which promises greater access speeds and full-screen, full-motion video without image degradation.

PC-based systems The dramatic burgeoning of the CD-ROM market has made this form of the optical disc familiar to all library staffs and users in the last few years. The convenience of being able to concentrate 250,000 sides of A4 text onto a 12-cm disc and, at the same time, provide automated searching of the text makes this format almost ideal for storing and searching reference information. Latterly, the illustrative features of such works as newspapers and encyclopedias, for example, have demonstrated the potential of CD-ROM to provide pictorial as well as textual information. The version of CD known as CD+G (Compact Disc plus Graphics) can also be mentioned here since it is an extension of the CD-ROM to provide animation rather than still illustrations.

A further development is Sony's CD-ROM XA (CD-ROM Extended Architecture), another multimedia system which provides sound and animation simultaneously, but motion video occupies only a portion of the screen and is at 15 frames/sec. There are no clear indications that the system will have applications for databases of still images, but where moving sequences are to be found this always suggests that there is potential for still picture storage. This has been realized more fully by the system known as DVI (Digital Video Interactive) developed by Intel and backed by IBM, Olivetti and Microsoft. This is aimed at business/educational users rather than the domestic market and currently provides 72 minutes of TV quality pictures, 650,000 pages of text, 44 hours of audio and storage for 40,000 still pictures. Again the system has developed as an add-on hardware card to the PC. As the majority of libraries already possess PCs this makes systems which extend their capabilities attractive options, both in terms of compatibility and costs.

Digital Compact Disc (Write Once Read Many systems)
Although the RO media have their advantages as secure library materials since the data cannot be erased or altered, it is the WORM systems which can more effectively simulate or possibly directly meet more exactly the requirements of a working image collection. The ability to progressively write or capture images of the library's choosing to an optical disc is the same process as accumulating or building any unique library collection of items.

This process is at present possible at reasonable working cost through Philips' and Kodak's Photo-CD system. This has direct application to existing slide collections since slide images can not only be transferred to the optical disc, but also regenerated from the disc. Clearly, the more robust nature of the CD medium can be of great value in preserving fragile slide images which have always been vulnerable to loss or damage during use. The ability to replace lost, faded, dirty or damaged images is an advantage which most slide collection managers would appreciate. Photo-CD is not only of use for preservation, however, but also gives rapid access to images and the ability to zoom in, that is, enable part of the original image to fill the television screen. The picture can also be rotated in its own plane on the screen. Although the figure of 100 images per disc appears low for library purposes, CD drives can be combined so that up to 100 discs can be accessed. Remote control access to 10,000 images can thus be achieved. Image capture can be from both print or transparent image and in effect a digital negative is stored on the disc. The higher specification system is called Portfolio CD. Gartner reports on using Photo-CD as part of the considerations to digitize images at the Bodleian Library.[2] Possibly Photo-CD has an immediate appeal and application for transferring slide stocks to CD under present market and technological conditions.

Compact disc standards

The rapidity of change and development in the computer, CD and multimedia world make it necessary for the student and others to keep up to date by scanning relevant journals. One of the key underlying aspects of how ways forward are effected is by the agreement of industry standards which come about by the collaboration and agreement of the large multinational concerns involved. Standards essentially are concerned with compatibility so that any CD a customer obtains will play on any manufacturer's player.

It is beyond the scope of this work to detail the technicalities involved with standards, but the following information is useful as a basis for following future developments which will continue to shape how still-image storage, retrieval and display will be formulated.

The colour book standards and the categories of the technology they refer to are as follows:

Red book   CD Digital Audio

Yellow book   CD-ROM and CD-ROM XA

Green book   CD Interactive

Orange book   New types of writable CD
                e.g. Photo-CD
                        CD Magneto Optical

Other acronyms to be aware of are JPEG (the Joint Picture Experts Group) which is involved in standards for the compression of still images and MPEG (the Motion Picture Experts Group) which is concerned with the corresponding standards for video compression.

Copyright of images
As always there are, quite properly, legal copyright obligations, responsibilities and restrictions which have to be honoured. However, the legally-framed relationship between copyright holders, libraries, material users and their respective representative bodies allows room for licensing agreements to be drawn up which can provide for the interests of creators/publishers and effective access for users.

Negotiations with respect to picture copying essentially involves establishing agreed codes of practice which protect creators without unduly stifling the free flow of information for non-profit-making educational use or legitimate private research purposes. Clearly, this is not an easy undertaking, but it is incumbent on creators, information providers and end users to respect the rights of other parties since their interests are ultimately interdependent. The need to safeguard the livelihood of photographers was embodied in the latest legislation (the Copyright, Designs and Patents Act 1988) and it has to be recognized that any threat to the creative process by extensive copying for profit-making purposes ultimately tends to impoverish all involved in image collection, appreciation and use. The 1988 Act in protecting the rights of photographers and publishers appeared to make illegal the copying of illustrations from books without first seeking the specific permission of the copyright holder. Copying of this nature had previously been a legitimate source of acquisition for academic slide libraries and the restriction has both proved onerous and damaging to academic interests.[3] There has been strong reaction from the Art Historian's Association and ARLIS/UK and Ireland to the situation.[4] Discussions continue between these bodies on the one hand and the Copyright Licensing Authority (CLA) and the Design and Artists' Copyright Society (DACS) on the other. It now appears likely that licensing agreements should be established during 1995.[5]

In the medical field the majority of slides are usually created in-house and, therefore, copyright rests with the hospital or medical school and their obligations to patients' rights. Naturally, copyright becomes more of a live issue when medical slides are offered for use outside the originating institution. A more urgent legal consideration in the medical slide context is the respect for patients' rights of confidentiality, especially when republication of medical illustrations is involved. This is dealt with more fully in Chapter 7 on the management of medical slides.

The rapid changes in imaging technology outlined above makes the copyright issue one which is unlikely to disappear in the foreseeable future. The proliferation of images in electronic formats, the ability to manipulate and edit existing images, the development of vast image databases and the transmission of images via networked computers are all set to compound copyright clearance considerations and their enforcement. Slides will continue to be involved in such matters as long as conventional photography remains at the base of the image creation superstructure and for as long as slide collections are maintained as original source material.

The standardization and integration of electronic communication networks into one unified system has been proposed and is set to have a far-reaching impact on the transmission and exchange of images should it be implemented successfully. The system known as Integrated Services Digital Networks (ISDN) involves all kinds of telecommunication transmissions including facsimile transmission, telephone, videophone, slow scan television and computer link-ups. Moving and still pictures will form part of the overall provision.[6] Legal control of images will, therefore, need constant adjustment to keep pace with such advances. For further study and reference on the difficulties of copyright, see the excellent analytical and practical work of R.A. Wall.[7]

Image displays

The optical disc systems covered in previous sections indisputably represent the most dramatic change in image creation, storage, retrieval and editing since the development of conventional photography. Although technological revolution is either announced or predicted almost daily there is no doubt that many of the difficulties presented by pictorial information in libraries will be significantly met by the new imaging technologies allied to computer retrieval. However, the image presented to the user can only be as good as that which the display unit or television screen is able to produce. Although the composition, editing and retrieval technology and techniques may be sophisticated, and selection may be from a vast bank of images, the final image must be of sufficient quality and definition for the client's purposes. Clearly, as mentioned earlier client's demands vary and the art historian has different demands than the advertiser.

Other important considerations concerning the image received from VDUs or television receivers is the perception of the viewer, the psychology of image perception or appreciation of the image by the brain coupled with the optical capabilities of the human eye. The nature of human colour vision remains imperfectly understood and differing theories exist. The complexity of this subject is well investigated and reported by Ester in a thorough examination of this area.[8]

High definition television (HDTV) exists at present, but has not been launched on the European market. At around £3–4,000 for a 36-inch set, costs will need to fall before sales on a mass scale take place. Uniform standards have yet to be finalized to enable manufacturers to commit themselves to volume production. Whereas conventional television has 625 lines and a screen dimension ratio (aspect ratio) of 4:3, HDTV has 1250 lines and an aspect ratio of 16:9. Screens can be up to 56-inch (measured across the diagonal). It is useful to note that the Philips Photo-CD system which is perhaps the system which has the greatest immediate potential for use with existing slide collections, is compatible with present Philips HDTV systems.

The application of HDTV allied to Photo-CD would be to compete with the conventional slide projector and screen in presenting images to groups. High resolution computer monitors are the other major way in which images in the future are likely to be displayed. It is important for slide managers to be clear that HDTV and computer monitors should not be directly compared for their resolution or definition qualities. Eccles and Romans[9] clarify the design aims and uses of HDTV and high resolution displays. They point out the different respective intentions of HDTV and computer display monitors and how the screens are designed to be viewed at different distances and in differing surrounding light conditions.

Clearly, viewer perception of the definition of an image is dependent on a number of interrelated variables such as the number of pixels or lines making up a picture the size of the screen, the viewing distance and distortion due to the curvature of screens. Suffice it to say that at present, quality colour slide film has considerably greater definition than television or computer monitor images with the larger film formats having the equivalent of 4,000 line television resolution.

9 Some principles of slide library management

The literature of slide management as a whole refrains from dog-matically asserting any distinct and separate principles of slide librarianship. However, in such substantial works as Irvine's and others it is implicit that the slide as a library format deserves special treatment and attention in order that it may realize its full potential. Indeed lack of special care or significant adjustment of the techniques used to manage other library formats to the needs of slide collections leads to waste and failure to meet potential clients' needs.

As has been mentioned previously it is the slide collection composed of unitary images which is the main concern and which forms the 'authentic' slide library. From all that has been written about the slide, and the now long-established existence of substantial collections in different subject fields, it is not untimely for some basic statements to be made which attempt to define the unique nature of slide librarianship. Again, as the foregoing chapters have indicated, the challenges to slide collec-tion management posed by optical disc and image database developments are another factor destined to alter our appreciation of pictorial storage and the place of existing slide collections in the appreciation of slide managers and users.

The principles

1 The slide is a visual format and as such falls within the province of picture librarianship. Its management requires an understanding of the visual image as a communication medium and as an information item.

Many collections exist which would not be considered as having connections with formal librarianship. In the commercial sphere for example, links with professional library bodies are not as strong as the academic, visual arts field. Nevertheless, the wider connotations of picture librarianship encompasses all slide collections irrespective of individuals' perceptions of their roles or differing views of the precise extent of the profession. Some theoretical study of pictures, as opposed to text, as carriers of information has to be undertaken to appreciate the nature and significance of illustrations to the user.

2 The slide library composed of discrete individual images requires recognition as a specialized library collection as distinct from a collection of tape/slide programmes or a packaged sequence of slides in a set.
3 As a visual format the slide requires the direct approach of browsing. This is usually best provided for by a classified arrangement.

With illustrations there is no substitute for directly viewing the images required. All techniques designed to help the user be they storage methods, indexes or key word searches are all directed to bringing about this all important contact between the eye of the user and the individual image. The importance of placing related images in close proximity, to further the process of browsing, can hardly be overestimated in the majority of collections.

4   The chosen storage method of slides, their arrangement within storage and their retrieval are closely interrelated and these three features cannot be successfully managed separately.

Much has been said in this work and others concerning the complexities covered by this principle. Perhaps more large-scale research needs to be carried out before more precise principles can be drawn up.

5   Since the possible approaches to pictorial material are manifold and the slide often requires indexing by many terms. Automated methods are strongly desirable to provide effective retrieval.
6   Each slide needs to carry information which determines its place within the storage arrangement and briefly describes the illustration. An indicator of the correct positioning of the slide for projection is a practical necessity.

Practical matters such as this may seem obvious particularly to those with experience of working with slides, but their neglect can prove fatal to the efficient running of a collection and a policy is required for working slide collections.

Bibliography

Albiges, Luce-Marie. Remote public access to picture databanks. *Audiovisual Librarian*, 18 (1992) 1, 22–27.

Allason-Jones, Lindsay. The case for BAPLA membership. *BAPLA Journal*, 1 (1994) 15.

Ames, Lynda. Equal pay for work of comparable value: issues to consider when beginning an initiative. *Visual Resources*, 6 (1990) 401–14.

Anglo-American cataloguing rules. 2nd edn. London: Library Association (1978).

Annual review of information science and technology. New York: Knowledge Industry Publications Inc. Annual.

ARLIS/NA-MACAA Visual resources subcommittee on slide quality. Statement on slide quality standards. *ARLIS/NA newsletter*, 6 (1978) 26–27.

ARLIS/UK and EIRE. ARLIS working party on standards and guidelines. *Guidelines for art and design libraries: stock, planning, staffing and autonomy*. ARLIS/UK and EIRE, 1990. Review – *Art libraries journal*, 16 (1991) 2, 33–36.

Armstrong, C.J. and Large, J.A. eds. *CD-ROM information products*. Aldershot: Ashgate Publishing (1990–92). 3 vols.

Art and architecture thesaurus (AAT). New York; Oxford: Oxford University Press for the Getty Art History Information Programme (1990) 3 vols. Also available on floppy disc as *The Authority Reference Tool* Edition. OUP (1993). Review – *Art Libraries Journal*. 16 (1991) 2, 29–33.

Art Libraries Journal. London: ARLIS/UK and Ireland (1978 to date). Quarterly.

Art libraries news-sheet. London: ARLIS/UK and Ireland (1969 to date). Six per year.

Ashby, P. Illustrated reference teaching and beyond: the microfiche approach. *Microform Review*, 8 (1979) 198–201.

Askham, David. *Photo libraries and agencies*. London: BFP Books (1990).

Audiovisual. London: EMAP Maclaren (1972 to date). Monthly.

Audiovisual directory. London: EMAP Maclaren. Annual.

Audiovisual librarian. London: Library Association and Aslib AV groups (1973 to date). Quarterly.

Austin, D. *PRECIS: a manual of concept analysis and subject indexing*. London: British Library (1984).

Babbitt, K.M. Indexing art slides. Term Paper. New Paltz, New York State University, School of Library Science (1968).

Bakewell, H.E. and Schmitt, M. *Object, image, inquiry: the art historian at work*. Santa Monica: J. Paul Getty Trust (1988).

BAPLA journal. London: British Association of Picture Libraries and Agencies (1984 to date). Quarterly.

Barker, V.F. Audio-visual stock and services. In Carmel, M. (ed.) *Medical Librarianship*. London: Library Association (1981). 126–30.

Barker, V.F. and Harden, R.M. MAVIS a medical audiovisual aids information service. *Journal of Audiovisual Media in Medicine*, 2 (1979) 60–63.

Barker, V.F. and Harden, R.M. *The storage and retrieval of 35mm slides*. Dundee: Association for the study of medical education (1980). Medical Education Booklet 11.

Barnett, Patricia J. The art and architecture thesaurus as a faceted MARC format. *Visual Resources*, 4 (1987) 247–59.

Beam, Philip C. Color slide controversy. *College Art Journal*. 2 (1943) 35–38.

Berry, Nicola. Information without limit. *PC Magazine*, 1 (Dec. 1992) 9, 229–55.

Betz, Elisabeth W. (comp.). *Graphic materials: rules for describing original items and historical collections*. Washington DC: Library of Congress (1982).

Bibliography of museum and art gallery publications and audiovisual aids in Great Britain and Northern Ireland. 2nd edn. Cambridge: Chadwyck-Healey (1980).

Bird, R.W. Slides: The cataloguing, classification and indexing of a collection of slides. *Catalogue and Index*, (1970) 4, 4.

Bird, R.W. The slide collection of Ravensbourne College of Art and Design. In Aslib audiovisual group. *Slides and sound recordings: their organisation and exploitation*. London: Aslib (1972). 50–55.

Bliss, H.E. *Bliss bibliographic classification*. 2nd edn. London: Butterworth (1977).

Boerner, S.Z. Slide library basics. *Texas Library Journal*, 54 (1978) 178–79.

Bogar, C.S. Classification for an architecture and art slide collection. *Special Libraries*, 66 (1975) 570–74.

Bradfield, V.J. *Slide collections: a user requirement survey*. Leicester: Leicester Polytechnic (1976). BLRD report 5309.

Bradfield, V.J. Slides and their users: thoughts following a survey of some slide collections in Britain. *Art Libraries Journal*, 2 (1977) 3, 4–21.

Bradshaw, D.N. and Hahn, C. *World photography sources*. Bowker (1983).

Brandhorst, Hans and Huisstede, Peter van. Report on the Iconclass workshop, June 26–28 1989. *Visual Resources*, 8 (1990) 1, 1–78.

Bridgman, C.F. and Suter, E. Searching AVLINE for curriculum-related audiovisual instructional materials. *Journal of Medical Education*, 54, (1979) 236–37.

Brink, A. (ed.). *Libraries, museums and art galleries yearbook*. Cambridge: James Clarke (1981).

British Association of Picture Libraries and Agencies. *BAPLA directory 1992–93*. London: BAPLA (1992).

British catalogue of audiovisual materials. London: British Library (1979).

British journal of photography. London: Henry Greenwood. Weekly.

British national bibliography (BNB). London: British Library (1950 to date). Weekly with monthly and annual cumulations.

British national film and video catalogue. London: British Film Institute (1984–1993). Quarterly with annual cumulations.

British national film catalogue. London: British Film Institute (1963–1983). Quarterly with annual cumulations.

British Standards Institution. *Universal decimal classification.* English full edition. London: BSI (1943). BS 1000.

British Standards Institution. *Specification for slides and film strips.* London: BSI (1968). BS 1917.

Brown, R.A.G., Fawkes, R.S. and Swanson Beck, J. Indexing and filing of pathological illustrations. *Journal of Clinical Pathology,* 28 (1975) 77–79.

Brumm, E.K. Optical disc technology for information management. In Williams, M.E.(ed.) *Annual review of information science and technology.* New York: Knowledge Industry Publications. Inc. Vol. 26 (1991). 197–240.

Bullard, J.E. (comp.). Slide collection: a catalogue of the 2 × 2" slides in the Library Association. *Library Information Bulletin,* (1973) 21, 25–62.

Carmel, M. (ed.). *Medical librarianship.* London: Library Association (1981).

Carpenter, James M. Limitations of color slides. *College Art Journal,* 2 (1943) 38–40.

Cashman, Norine D. *Slide buyers guide: an international directory of slide sources for art and architecture.* 6th edn. Englewood, Colorado: Libraries Unlimited (1990).

Chadwyck-Healey, C. Microforms. In Harrison, H.P (ed.) *Picture Librarianship.* London: Library Association (1981) 161.

Chater, Kathy. *The television researcher's guide.* Boreham Wood: BBC Television Training (1989).

Cilliers, J.M. Organisation of a slide collection in a medical library. *Medical Library Association Bulletin,* 69 (1981) 330–33.

Clark, David R. Semantic descriptors and maps of meaning for videodisc images. *Programmed Learning and Educational technology,* 23,1 (1986) 84–89.

Clark, W. R. and Harrison, K. Lanslide: the automation of the University of Lancaster Library's slide collection. *Audiovisual Librarian,* 14 (1988) 4, 196–200.

Clawson, C.R. and Rankowski, C.A. Classification and cataloguing of slides using color photocopying. *Special Libraries,* 69 (1978) 281–85.

Clawson, C.R. and Rankowski, C.A. Slide classification and cataloguing: further considerations. *Special Libraries,* 72 (1981) 39–43.

Cockburn, N. Slide retrieval systems a pharmaceutical industry approach. *Journal of Audiovisual Media in Medicine*, 5 (1982) 27–29.

Collins, Donna Lacy. A slide library data base using the Apple Macintosh plus system. *Visual Resources*, V (1988) 2, 135–50. (Describes automation of the George Washington University art slide department at Washington DC.)

Commodore Dynamic Total Vision, CDTV interactive TV systems. *British Journal of Photography*, 138 (6 June 1991) 3.

Computers in the history of art. (CHART). New York: Harwood Academic (1991 to date). 2 per year.

Coulson, A.J. Conference report: slides, their acquisition and organisation. *ARLIS Newsletter*, (1975) 23, 32–33.

Coulson, A.J. Picture libraries: a survey of the present situation and a look into the future. *INSPEL*. 22 (1988) 3, 190–95. Reprinted in *Audiovisual Librarian*, 15 (1989) 2, 99–102.

Couprie, L.D. *Iconclass:* a device for the iconographical analysis of art objects. *Museum*, 314 (1978) 30, 194–98.

Couprie, L.D. *Iconclass*: an iconographic classification system. *Art Libraries Journal*, 8 (1983) 2, 32–49.

Croghan, A.J. The problem of making a modern indexing language for the Fine Arts. *ARLIS Newsletter*, (1974) 20, 26–31.

Danziger, Pamela N. Picture databases: a practical approach to picture retrieval. *Database*, 13 (1990) 4, 13–17.

Darling, L. (ed.). *Handbook of medical library practice.* 4th edn. Chicago: American Library Association (1983).

Davis, M. Computerised visual indexes: a review. *Drexel Library Quarterly*, 8 (1972) 173–79.

Davis, R. The professional status of slide curators. *ARLIS Newssheet*, no. 55 (1985) 3–5.

DeBardeleben, M.Z. and Lunsford, C.G. 35mm slides: storage and retrieval for the novice. *Special Libraries*, 73 (1982) 135–41.

Decimal Index of Art in the Low Countries (DIAL). This is a series of postcard sized photographs of Netherlands works of art arranged according to ICONCLASS order. The publication of the cards is a joint enterprise of the Department of Art History at the University of Leiden and the Netherlands Institute for the History of Art.

Delaurier, N. Slide collections outside North America – Survey on major features of 36 collections. *International Bulletin for Photographic Documentation of the Visual Arts*, 9 (1982) 4, 11. Supplement.

Delaurier, N. Visual resources: the state of the art. *Art Libraries Journal*, 7 (1982) 3, 7–21.

Dewey, Melvil. *Dewey decimal classification and relative index*. 20th edn. Albany New York: Forest Press, 4 vols.

Dewey, Melvil. Library pictures. *Public Libraries*, 11 (1906) 10.

Diamond, R. *The development of a retrieval system for 35mm slides utilised in art and humanities instruction*. Fredonia, New York: State University College of New York at Fredonia (1969).

Diamond, R. A retrieval system for 35mm slides utilised in art and humanities instruction. In. Grove, P.S. and Clement, E.G. (eds). *Bibliographical control of non print media*. Chicago: American Library Association, (1972). 346–59.

Doran, M. and Phillpot, C. Chelsea School of Art – an art school library classification. *ARLIS Newsletter*, (1970) 5, 2–5.

Duffield, Rachel. Proposals for a slide library licensing scheme. *Audiovisual Librarian*, 19 (1993) 4, 285–86.

Eakins, Rosemary, (ed.). *Picture sources UK*. London: Macdonald (1985).

Eccles, David and Romans, Gary. High definition vs high resolution displays: what sort of image quality? *Advanced Imaging*, Sept (1992) 16–20; 81.

Editorial: Iconclass projects. *Visual Resources*, 7 (1990) 1, vii–xiii.

Editorial: Iconclass at forty. *Visual Resources*, 8 (1991) 1, vii–x.

Educational Products Information Centre. *Educational software selector*. Teacher's College Press (1988).

Ellis, Shirley. A thousand words about the slide. *ALA Bulletin*, 53 (1959) 529–32.

Ellison, J.W. *Films, filmstrips, filmloops, transparencies and slides: storage and care self-evaluation form*. Buffalo: State University of New York. School of Information and Library Studies (1978).

Ely, Donald P. and Minor, Barbara B. (eds). *Educational media and technology yearbook*. Englewood, Colorado: Libraries Unlimited, annual.

English, B. and Willey, E.N. A storage and retrieval system for projection slides. *Journal of Biological Photography*, 35 (1967) 60–64.

Ester, Michael. Image quality and viewer perception. *Visual Resources*, 7 (1991) 4, 327–52.

Evans, Grace E. and Stein, Lenore. Image-bearing catalog cards for photo-libraries: an overview and a proposal. *Special libraries*, 70 (1979) 11, 462–70.

Evans, Hilary. *The art of picture research. A guide to current practice, procedure, techniques and resources*. Newton Abbot: David and Charles (1979).

Evans, Hilary and Evans, Mary. (comps.). *Picture researcher's handbook*. London: Chapman and Hall, 5th edn (1992).

Excerpta Medical Foundation. *Excerpta Medica*. Amsterdam: Excerpta Medical Foundation. Monthly.

Fennell, Y. Chester photographic survey. *Library Association Record*, 72 (1970) 197–99.

Foolproof slide cataloguing system. *Petersen's Photographic Magazine*, 6 (1978) 56–57.

Foskett, A.C. *The subject approach to information*. 4th edn. London: Bingley (1982).

Fothergill, Richard and Butchart, Ian. *Non-book materials in libraries*. 3rd edn. London: Bingley (1990).

Freeman, Carla Conrad. Visual media in education: an informal history. *Visual Resources*, 6 (1990) 327–40.

Freeman, Carla Conrad. Visual collections as information centres. *Visual Resources*, 6 (1990) 349–60.

Freeman, Carla Conrad. Professional Issues for the visual resources curator: a bibliography. *Visual Resources*, 6 (1990) 415–22.

Freitag, W. The early uses of photography in the history of art. *Art Journal*, 39 (1979/80) 117–123.

Freitag, W.M. Slides for individual use in the College Library. *Library Trends*, 23 (1975) 495–99.

Freitag, W.M. and Irvine, B.J. Slides. In Grove, P.S. (ed.) *Non print media in academic libraries*. Chicago: American Library Association (1975) 102–21.

Freudenthal, J.R. The slide as a communication tool. *School Media Quarterly*, 2 (1974) 112.

Freudenthal, J.R. *The slide as a communication tool: A selective bibli-*

ography. 2nd edn. Boston, Mass: Simmons College, School of Library Science (1974).

Gartner, Richard. Digitising the Bodleian? *Audiovisual Librarian*, 19 (1993) 3, 220–23.

Gerrard, J. Laser looking fast. *Guardian*, 12 May 1988.

Gilley, B. Declassifying the slide secrets. *Museum News*, 53 (1974) 45–48.

Gilson, C.C. and Collins, J.M. Use of a microcomputer in a department of medical illustration for retrieval of clinical teaching slides. *Journal of Audiovisual Media in Medicine*, 5 (1982) 130–34.

Godfrey, J. A slide library as a teaching resource in art and design education: improving slide retrieval for users. *Audiovisual Librarian*, 15 (1989) 4, 190–200.

Godfrey, J. The visual imagery used in the teaching of art and design: problems of acquisition for the slide librarian. *Audiovisual Librarian*, 17 (1991) 2, 90–94.

Gordon, Catherine. Report on the *Iconclass* workshop November 2–4, 1987. *Visual Resources*, 5 (1988) 3, 197–258.

Grant, Cathy. (ed.). *Distributors: the guide to video and film sources for education and training*. London: BUFVC (1990).

Green, S.J. *The classification of pictures and slides*. Denver, Col.: Little Books (1984).

Greenhalgh, Michael. Videodisks and their future in art history. *Visual Resources*, 6 (1989) 2.

Grove, P.S. (ed.). *Nonprint media in academic libraries*. Chicago: American Library Association (1975).

Guide to government departments and other libraries. London: British Library. Bienniel.

Gunn, Angela A. and Moore, Caroline (eds). *CD-ROM a practical guide for information professionals*. London: UKOLUG/Library & Information Technology Centre (1990).

Gunn, M.J. Colour microforms and their application to the visual arts. *Microform Review*, 8 (1979) 187–92.

Gunther, A. Slides in documentation. *Unesco Bulletin for Libraries*, 17 (1963) 157–63.

Gustafson, Karen. Slide circulation survey report. *Visual Resources Association Bulletin*, 18 (1991) 2, 28–32.

Harden, R.M. Indexing audiovisual aids on a feature card system. *Medical and Biological Illustration*, 18 (1968) 263–67.

Harden, R.M. Presentation of patient management problems using a random access slide projector. *Journal of Audiovisual Media in Medicine*, 5 (1982) 72–74.

Harden, R.M., Harden, R.K., Jolley, J. and Wilkin, T.J. Punched feature card systems in clinical research. *British Journal of Hospital Medicine*, 13 (1975) 195.

Harris, S. The organisation of slide libraries. *Construction Industry Information Review*, (1977–78) 2, 22–23.

Harrison, H.P. Non-book materials: a decade of development? *Journal of Documentation*, 35 (1979) 207–48.

Harrison, H.P. (ed.). *Picture librarianship*. London: Library Association (1981).

Harrison, Ken. and Clark, Winifred R. Lanslide – the development of a system for managing a slide collection at the University of Lancaster Library. *Program*, 22 (1988) 4, 365–77.

Havard-Williams, P. and Karling, S.A. *Rules for the cataloguing of slides in the Liverpool School of Architecture* (unpublished list).

Havard-Williams, P. and Watson, S. The slide collection at Liverpool School of Architecture. *Journal of Documentation*, 16 (1960) 11–14.

Hedley, A.J. and Morton, R. The clinical slide library: a valuable learning resource in continuing medical education. *Medical and Biological Illustration*, 26 (1976) 203–07.

Hess, S.W. *An annotated bibliography of slide library literature*. Bibliographic Studies, no. 3. Syracuse: Syracuse University, New York, School of Information Studies (1978).

Higgott, A. *The Architectural Association Slide Library*. London: The Architectural Association (1980).

Hoffman, S. and Simon, B.E. A filing system for transparencies. *Annals of Plastic Surgery*, 1 (1978) 330–32.

Holmes, R. Laser disc technology: the implications for medicine and medical information. *Audiovisual Librarian*, 14 (1988) 4, 201–10.

Hoort, Rebecca Miller. Equal pay for equal work and comparable worth: an introduction. *Visual Resources*, 6 (1990) 399–400.

Hoort, Rebecca Miller. (ed.). Professionalism. *Visual Resources*, 6 (1990) 315–422.

Hoover, S.R. Slide and photograph collections: the shoe box days are over. *American Libraries*, 10 (1979) 440–41.

Hospitals and health services yearbook. London: Institute of Health Services Management. Annual.

Hourdajian, A. Developments in color micrographics. *Microform Review*, 12 (1983) 161–62.

Hyland, Gareth. Medical illustration: resource efficiency. *British Journal of Photography*, (13 September 1990) 6786, 22–23.

Iconclass: iconographic classification. Amsterdam, Leiden and Utrecht: Iconclass research and development group, 1973–85.

Institute of Medical and Biological Illustration. *Directory of members*. Unpublished list.

International yearbook of educational and training technology. London: Kogan Page. Annual.

Irvine, Betty Jo. Slide collections in art libraries. *College and research libraries*, 30 (1969) 443–45.

Irvine, Betty Jo. Slide classification: a historical survey. *College and research libraries*, 32 (1971) 23–30.

Irvine, Betty Jo. Organisation and management of art slide collections. *Library Trends*, 23 (1975) 401–16.

Irvine, Betty Jo. *Slide libraries: a guide for academic institutions, museums, and special collections*. 2nd edn. Littleton, Colorado: Libraries Unlimited (1979).

Irvine, Betty Jo. (ed.). *Facilities standards for art libraries and visual resources collections*. Englewood, Colorado: Libraries Unlimited (1991).

Jones, M.C. *International guide to locating audio-visual materials in the health sciences*. Aldershot: Gower (1986).

Journal of Audiovisual Media in Medicine. Guildford: Butterworth-Heinemann (1976 to date). Quarterly.

Keeling, Derek. A century of 35mm. *British Journal of Photography*, (14 March 1991) 6811, 29–31.

Kemp, Martin. The making of slides from illustrations in books, periodicals etc. *Art Historians Bulletin*, (1991) 35, 32.

Kessler, Benjamin R. Professional qualifications: where do we come from? What are we? Where are we going? *Visual Resources*, 6 (1990) 367–78.

Kirby, John. Slides, microfilms, microfiches. In. Pearce, M. (ed.).

Non-standard collection management. Aldershot: Ashgate (1992) 196–210.

Kirkpatrick, N. Major issues of the past ten years in visual resources curatorship. *Art Libraries Journal*, 7 (1982) 4, 30–35.

Kodak's Photo-CD system takes its bow. *The Photographic Journal*, 130 November 1990,485.

Kodak. *The storage and care of Kodak photographic materials before and after processing*. Hemel Hempstead: Kodak (1992).

Kohn, L.E. A photograph and lantern slide catalogue in the making. *Library Journal*, 57 (1932) 941–45.

Krause, M.G. Intellectual problems of indexing picture collections. *Audiovisual Librarian*, 14 (1988) 73–81.

Kuvshinoff, B.W. A graphic graphics card catalogue and computer index. *American Documentation*, 18 (1967) 3–9.

Lambert, Steve and Sallis, Jane. (eds). *CD-I and interactive videodisc technology*. Indianapolis: Sams (1987).

Langford, M. *The story of photography: from its beginnings to the present day*. London: Focal Press (1980).

Larsen, John C. (ed.). *Museum librarianship*. Hamden, Connecticut: Library Professional Publications (1985).

Lea, P.W. (ed.). *Printed reference material*. 3rd edn. London: Library Association (1990).

Lemke, A.B. Slide librarianship: a contemporary survey. *ARLIS/NA News*, (1975) 85.

Lemke, A.B. Education and training. In. Harrison, H.P. (ed.). *Picture librarianship*. London: Library Association (1981) 228–39.

Lewis, E.M. A graphic catalogue card index. *American Documentation*, 20 (1969) 238–46.

Lewis, E.M. Control without cards: the organisation of colour slide collections without card references. *ARLIS/NA Newsletter*, 1 (1973) 17.

Library of Congress. Subject cataloguing division. *Library of Congress classification*. Washington, DC: Library of Congress (1917).

Lo Presti, M. An automated slide classification system at Georgia Tech. *Special Libraries*, 64 (1973) 509–13.

Logan, Anne-Marie. *British artists authority list, from the Yale centre for British art photograph archive.* VRA Special bulletin no. 1. Arkansas: VRA (1992).

McArthur, J.R. The American Society of Hematology slide bank. In *Hematology/Hematologic/Transfusion.* Montreal: American Society of Hematology (1980) 110–16.

MacCallum, Ann. The organisation of slide collections: a view from the Canberra Institute of Arts. *ARLIS/ANZ News,* September 1989, 28, 9–14.

McKeneney, Kathryn K. Winterthur museum. *Visual Resources Association Bulletin,* 17 (1990) 2, 23–27.

McKenna, M. Regional av services. In Tabour, R.B. (ed.). *Libraries for health: the Wessex experience.* Southampton: Wessex Regional Library and Information Service (1978) 115–16.

McKeown, Roy. *National directory of slide collections.* London: British Library (1990). British Library information guide 12.

McKeown, Roy. Slides as information materials: the national survey of slide collections. *Audiovisual Librarian,* 16 (1990) 3, 127–31.

McKeown, Roy. The National Art Slide Library: a developing picture. *Audiovisual librarian,* 18 (1992) 4, 252–54.

McKeown, Roy. The Centre for Image Information: the shape of things to come. *Art Libraries Journal,* 18 (1993) 3, 28–31.

McKeown, Roy and Otter, Mary Edmunds. *National survey of slide collections.* London: British Library, 1989. British Library research paper 67.

McPherson, Alan and Timms, Howard. *The audio-visual handbook.* London: Pelham Books (1988).

McRae, Linda. Professionalism: report on the 1990 VR survey Part 1. *Visual Resources,* 17 (1990) 3, 6–8.

McRae, Linda. Upgrading professional status: Florida as a case study. *Visual Resources,* 6 (1990) 379–86.

McRae, Linda. Professionalism: report on the 1990 VR survey Part 2. *Visual Resources,* 17 (1990) 4, 6–8.

Maher, Ann. (ed.). *Software users year book 1994.* VNU Business Publications. 4 vols (1994).

Mannikka, Eleanor. *Selected topics in cataloguing Asian art.* VRA Special bulletin 4. Arkansas: VRA (1992).

Manning, Martha. SGAA slide collection. *Stained Glass Quarterly,* 84, Fall '89, 232.

Maran, A.G. Slides and the otolaryngologist. *Clinical Otolaryngology*, 9 (1984) 171–74.

Markey, Karen. Visual art resources and computers: slide collections. In Williams, M.E. (ed.). *Annual review of information science and technolog, vol. 19*. New York: Knowledge Industry Publications. Inc. 1984. 282–84.

Markey, Karen. *Subject access to visual resources collections*. New York and London: Greenwood Press. (1986).

Maslen, B. Slide loan service for Hertfordshire. *ARLIS Newsletter*, (1972) 10, 7–9.

Matthews, J. The slide library of the faculty of art and design of Bristol Polytechnic. *Art Libraries Journal*, 1 (1976) 4, 20–25.

Matthews, J. *Library organisation of audio visual materials and equipment for the user*. Aberystwyth: College of Librarianship Wales (1977). Student Project 9.

Matthews, Robert. When seeing is not believing. *New Scientist*, (1993) 1895, 13–15.

Maxwell, B. The National Art slide library at the Victoria and Albert Museum. *Art Libraries Journal*, 2 (1977) 4, 31–36.

MDA Information. Cambridge: Museums Documentation Association. Quarterly.

The medical directory. London: Churchill. 2 vols. Annual.

The medical register. London: General Medical Council. 2 vols. Annual.

Mekkawi, M., Palmer, L.H. and Lons, W.W. Jr. *SLIDEX: A system for indexing, filing and retrieving slides and other visual aids*. Washington, DC.: Howard University (1978).

Merrett, C.E. Computerised information retrieval from a slide collection for architecture. *South African Libraries*, 47 (1980) 103–06.

Mid-America College Art Association. *Guide to management of visual resources collections*. New Mexico: MACCA (1979).

Milgrom, L. *On-line retrieval of clinical slides*. Paper presented at the annual meeting of the Medical Library Association: Chicago, Illinois, June 1978. Educational Resources Information Center Report ED 162631.

Mitchell, Joanne. (ed.). *The CD-ROM directory 1990*. 5th edn. London: TFPL Publishing (1991).

Molholt, Pat. The art and architecture thesaurus: a project report. *Visual Resources*, 1 (1980/81) 2/3, 193–99.

More, Jill. Slide collections. *ARLIS/ANZ News*, September 1989, 28, 15–18.

Morton, Richard. The image database: pictures and computers. *Journal of Audiovisual Media in Medicine*, 15 (1992) 2, 54–56.

Murray, P. Some problems of an art historian in a library. *ARLIS Newsletter*, (1975) 23, 4–7.

Murton, J. The Design Council slide library. *Art Libraries Journal*, 1 (1976) 4, 26–32.

Museum News. London: Museums Association. Monthly.

National Audiovisual Centre. *A reference list of audiovisual materials produced by the U.S. government*. Washington DC: National Audiovisual Centre, National Archives and records service (1978).

National Information Centre for Educational Media (NICEM). *Index to educational slides*. Los Angeles: NICEM, University of Southern California. 3rd edn (1977).

National Library of Medicine (NLM). *Index Medicus*. Bethesda Maryland: NLM, US Dept. of Health and Human Sciences (1960 to date). Monthly.

National Library of Medicine (NLM). *Medical subject headings (MeSH) used in Index Medicus*. Bethesda, Maryland: NLM, US Dept. of Health and Human Sciences. Annually.

National Library of Medicine (NLM). *NLM audiovisuals catalog*. Bethesda Maryland: NLM, US Dept. of Health and Human Sciences (1980).

National Library of Medicine (NLM). *NLM Classification*. NLM, Bethesda Maryland: US Dept. of Health and Human Sciences. 4th edn (1981).

National union catalog. Audiovisual materials. Washington DC: Library of Congress (1983 to date).

National union ctalog. Films and other materials for projection. Washington DC: Library of Congress (1973–79).

National union catalog. Motion pictures and filmstrips. Washington DC: Library of Congress (1953–62 and 1968–72).

Newhall, B. *The history of photography: from 1839 to the present day*. 4th edn, London: Secker and Warburg (1972).

Nichols, Chris. (comp.). *ARLIS union list of microforms on art, design and related subjects.* ARLIS/UK and EIRE (1988).

Nolan, M.P. The metropolitan museum of art slide library. In Mount, E. (ed.). *Planning the special library.* New York: New York Special Libraries Association (1972) 101–03.

Otey, Astrid R. A history of the Visual Resources Association. *Visual Resources,* 6 (1990) 341–48.

Pacey, P. Handling slides single-handed. *Art Libraries Journal,* 2 (1977) 3, 22–30.

Pacey, P. Slides and filmstrips. In Pacey, P. (ed.). *Art library manual: a guide to resources and practice.* London and New York: Bowker (1977) 272–84.

Pacey, Philip. National directory of slide collections. *Art Libraries Journal,* 15 (1990) 2, 49–51. (Review of the directory.)

Page, J.A. Slides in the public library. *ARLIS/NA Newsletter,* 4 (1976) 3, 84–85.

Panofsky, Erwin. *Meaning in the visual arts.* New York: Doubleday Anchor Books (1955).

Panofsky, Erwin. *Studies in iconology.* New York: Harper and Row (1962).

Payea, N.P. II and Mara J.E. A system for organizing and storing slides. *Annals of Plastic Surgery,* 10 (1983) 329–30.

Pearce, R. Functions of visuals in tape-slide instructional programmes. *Audiovisual Librarian,* 10 (1984) 18–23.

Pearman, Sara Jane. An opinion: mumblings of a slide librarian. *Art Documentation,* 7 (1988) 4, 145–46.

Perry, T. Slide: overcoming the anxieties. *Florida Media Quarterly,* 5 (1980) 9–11.

Pers, M. A system for storage of color slides. *Annals of Plastic Surgery,* 3 (1979) 474–79.

Perusse, L.F. Classifying and cataloguing lantern slides for the architecture library. *Journal of Cataloguing and Classification,* 10 (1954) 77–83.

Philip, G. ISDN: An emerging electronic highway for business data communication. *Journal of Information Science,* 19 (1993) 4, 279–89.

Pinion, Catherine F. Audiovisual materials. In Taylor, L.J. (ed.). *British library and information work 1976–1980.* London: Library Association (1983) vol. 2. 118–32.

Pinion, Catherine F. Preserving our audiovisual heritage: a national and international challenge. *Audiovisual Librarian*, 19 (1993) 3, 205–19.

Pohlmann, Ken C. *The compact disc handbook*. Oxford: Oxford University Press (1992).

Prakash, U.B. Filing and retrieval of a personal collection of 35mm teaching slides in medicine. *Archives of Internal Medicine*, 145 (1985) 1680–82.

Pring, Isobel. (ed.). *Image 89: The international meeting on museums and art galleries image databases*. London: Image (1990).

Program. London: Aslib. Quarterly.

Prytherch, R. (ed). *Harrod's librarian's glossary and reference book*. 7th edn. London: Gower (1990).

Ranganathan, S.R. *Colon classification*. 7th edn. New York: Asia Publishing House (1971).

Raymond, S.L. and Algermissen, V.L. A retrieval system for bio-medical slides using MeSH. *Medical Library Association Bulletin*, 64 (1976) 233–35.

Reinhardt, P.A. Photograph and slide collections in art libraries. *Special Libraries*, 50 (1959) 97–102.

Rhyne, Charles S. A slide collection of Constable's paintings: the art historian's need for visual documentation. *Visual Resources*, 4 (1987) 1, 51–70.

Roberts, Helen E. The visual document. *Art Libraries Journal*, 13 (1988) 2, 5–8.

Roberts, M. Slide collections: some retrieval problems and their solution. *Construction Industry Information Group Bulletin*, 1 (1970) 5–12.

Roberts, M. Organisation of slide collections in construction industry libraries. In Aslib audio visual group. *Slides and sound recordings: their organisation and exploitation*. London: Aslib (1972) 37–46.

Roberts, Stephen. Towards a pocket library. *Audiovisual Librarian*, 17 (1991) 2, 95–104.

Robinson, C.D. Indexing nonbook materials by PRECIS. In Wellish, H.H. *The PRECIS indexing system: principles, applications and prospects*. H.W. Wilson (1977) 169–74.

Robl, E. (ed.). *Picture sources 4*. New York: Special Libraries Association (1983).

Roddy, Kevin. Subject access to visual resources. *Library Hi Tech,* 9 (1991) 1, 45–49.

Rook, Sherrie. An ideal slide library reference shelf. *International Bulletin for Photographic Documentation in the Visual Arts,* 15 (1988) 4, 13–14.

Rowland, Melanie and Seeley, Maureen. Image databases – the facts of life. *Audiovisual Librarian,* 17 (1991) 4, 217–20.

Rush, J. Slide and photographic libraries. *Construction Industry Information Group Bulletin,* 4 (1974) 2, 3–4.

Saffady, William. *Optical disks vs micrographics as document storage and retrieval technologies.* London: Meckler (1988).

Saffady, William. *Optical disks vs magnetic storage.* London: Meckler (1990).

Saffady, William. *Optical storage technology 1992: A state of the art review.* London: Meckler (1992).

Samuel, E.K. Microforms and art libraries. *Microform Review,* 10 (1981) 141–47.

Savage, F. Two million transparencies. *Tropical doctor,* 10 (1980) 143–44.

Saxby, G. *The Focal guide to slides.* London: Focal Press (1979).

Schrock, N.C. Preservation and storage. In *Picture Librarianship.* London: Library Association (1981) 85–130.

Schuller, N. Slide collections. *Texas Library Journal,* 47 (1971) 208–10, 242.

Schuller, Nancy Shelby. *Management for visual resources collections.* 2nd edn. Englewood, Colorado: Libraries Unlimited (1989).

Schuller, Nancy Shelby. *Standard abbreviations for image descriptions for use in fine arts visual resources collections.* VRA Special Bulletin 2: Visual Resources Association (1989).

Schuller, Nancy Shelby. The curator's job description: development and evaluation. *Visual Resources,* 6 (1990) 387–92.

Scott, A. *The great slide show book.* London: Adam and Charles Black (1984).

Scott, Gillian. (ed.). *Guide to equipment for slide maintenance and viewing.* Albuquerque, New Mexico: MACAA (1978).

Seloff, Gary. VRMS: worth a second look. *Visual Resources Association Bulletin,* 17 (1990) 3, 14–16. (VRMS = Visual Resources Management System, a commercially available automation software package).

Sherman, Claire Richter. Iconclass: A historical perspective. *Visual Resources*, 4 (1987) 3, 237–46.

Shifrin, M. *Information in the school library: an introduction to the organisation of non-book materials.* London: Bingley (1973).

Siegel, D.E. Bibliography on slides. *Catholic Library World*, 48 (1977) 448–50.

Siertsema, J.V., Blanksma, L.J. and Timmerman, Z. Storage and retrieval of slides and angiograms. *Journal of Audiovisual Media in Medicine*, 3 (1980) 92–93.

Siertsema, J.V., Rose, J.H. and Blanksma, L.J. Management of a large ophthalmological slide collection. *Journal of Audiovisual Media in Medicine*, 6 (1983) 147–48.

Simons, W.W. Development of a universal classification system for two-by-two inch slide collections. In. Grove, P.S. and Clement, E.G. (eds). *Bibliographical control of nonprint media.* Chicago: American Library Association (1972) 360–73.

Simons, W.W. and Tansey, L.C. *A slide classification system for the organisation and automatic indexing of interdisciplinary collections of slides and pictures.* Santa Cruz: University of California (1970).

Sirkin, A.F. Recent technological developments. In Harrison, H.P. (ed.). *Picture librarianship.* London: Library Association (1981) 154–58.

Skoog, A. and Evans, G. A slide collection classification. *Pennsylvania Library Association Bulletin*, 24 (1969) 15–22.

Slater, P. The major slide collections in the libraries of the University of London. *Libraries Bulletin of the University of London*, (1978) 12, 4–7, 13.

Small, Jocelyn Penny. Retrieving images verbally. *Library Hi Tech*, 9 (1991) 1, 51–60.

Smith, C. Now 3-D slide shows are here. *Audio Visual*, (1982) 129, 94–95, 97.

Snow, Maryly. Visual depictions and the use of MARC: a view from the trenches of slide librarianship. *Art Documentation*, 8 (1989) 4, 186–87, 189–90.

Sorkow, J. Videodiscs and art documentation. *Art Libraries Journal*, 8 (1983) 3, 27–41.

Steadman, Stephen, Nash, Colin., and Eraut, Michael. *NCET CD-ROM in schools scheme. Evaluation report*. Coventry: NCET (1992).

Stern, N. Classifying, indexing and storing teaching slides. *Dental Radiography and Photography*, 46 (1973) 86–88.

Stewart, R.T. and Shapiro, M. A simple way to index, file and retrieve slides. *Dental Survey*, 46 (1970) 33–35.

Strohlein, A. *The management of 35mm medical slides*. New York: United Business Publications (1975).

Stubley, Peter and Umney, Darren. Multimedia. *Library and information briefings*, 34 (1992).

Sunderland, J. Photographic collections. *ARLIS Newsletter*, (1974) 19, 3–7.

Sunderland, J. Image collections: librarians, users and their needs. *Art Libraries Journal*, 7 (1982) 2, 41.

Sundt, Chistine L. Mounting slide film between glass – for preservation or destruction? *Visual Resources*, 2 (1981, 1982) 37–62.

Sundt, Christine L. *Conservation practices for slide and photograph collections*. VRA Special Bulletin 3. Visual Resources Association (1989).

Sundt, Christine L. Professionalism and professional status: personal reflections. *Visual Resources*, 6 (1990) 321–26.

Sutcliffe, G.S. *The management and exploitation of photographic slide collections in university teaching hospitals*. Unpublished M.Phil. thesis. Aberystwyth: University of Wales (1989).

Sutcliffe, G.S. Management of slides by departments of medical illustration and medical libraries in university teaching hospitals. *Journal of Audiovisual Media in Medicine*, 13 (1990) 4, 135–42.

Swan, E. Problems involved in establishing a slide collection in the School of Architecture, University of Melbourne. *Australian Library Journal*, 9 (1960) 159–62.

Tabour, R.B. The use of 35mm transparencies in the National Health Service. In Aslib audio visual group. *Slides and sound recordings: their organisation and exploitation*. London: Aslib (1972) 56–63.

Talking with slides: more than a half-way house. *Audio Visual*, 9 (1980) 28–30.

Tansey, L. Classification of research photographs and slides. *Library Trends*, 23 (1975) 417–26.

Tansey, L. and Simons, W. The computer at Santa Cruz: slide classification with automated cross-indexing. *Picturescope*, 18 (1979) 64–75.

Terris, Olwen. AVANCE: a multimedia database. *Audiovisual Librarian*, 16 (1990) 3, 113–15.

Thompson, A.H. Guidelines to achieve minimum standards of presentation for over-head transparencies and slides. *Audiovisual Librarian*, 5 (1979) 26–27.

Thompson, John (ed.). *Manual of curatorship: a guide to museum practice.* 2nd edn. London: Butterworth-Heinemann (1992).

Toyne, D. Requests at Falmouth School of Art. *ARLIS Newsletter*, (1975) 24, 17–18.

Trebble, A.E. *The impact of new media on libraries: a survey of present practice.* Brighton: University of Sussex Library (1973). OSTI report 5165.

Treese, W.R. Rephotographing microforms: the translation of microfiche and microfilm into slides and photographic prints. *Microform Review*, 12 (1983) 163–65.

Trenner, L. The growth of a slide library: The Courtauld Institute of Art. *Art Libraries Journal*, 8 (1983) 4, 23–28.

Tull, A.G. The conservation of colour photographic records. 3: Dimensional characteristics of some available slide mounts. *ARLIS Newsletter*, (1973) 17, 24–25.

UK national medical slide bank on videodisc. Cambridge and Chelmsford: Chadwyck-Healey and Graves Educational Resources. (1989). LaserVision videodisc.

Updike, Christina B. Position classification. *Visual Resources*, 6 (1990) 393–98.

Varley, Gillian. (ed.). *Art and design documentation in the United Kingdom and Ireland: a directory of resources.* London: ARLIS/UK (1993).

Viewfinder. London: British Universities Film and Video Council. 3 per year.

Viles, M. The slide collection, Edinburgh College of Art. *ARLIS Newsletter*, (1973) 17, 19–20.

Visser, O. The Stellenbosch University medical library slide classification, storage, retrieval and issue system. *Medical Library Association Bulletin*, 65 (1977) 377–79.

Visual arts information services handbook. Leeds: Axis, Leeds Polytechnic (1992).

Visual resources: an international journal of documentation. New York and Reading: Gordon and Breach (1980 to date). Quarterly.

VRA bulletin. Arkansas: Visual resources Association (1973 to date). Quarterly.

Waal, H. van de. In Couprie, L., Fuchs, R.H. and Tholen, E. (eds). *Iconclass: an iconographic classification system*. Amsterdam, North Holland Publishing Company (1974).

Wald, I. The evolution of the Cornell SPIRES slide indexing system. *Art Documentation*, 1 (1982) 13–15.

Walker, Lester C. Jnr. Slide filing and control. *College Art Journal*, 16 (1957) 325–29.

Wall, J. (comp.). *Directory of British photographic collections*. London: Heinemann (1977).

Walsh, P. *The microform image – substitute, facsimile or counterfeit*. College Art Association conference paper, February 25 1982.

Wasserman, M.N. A computer-prepared book catalogue for engineering transparencies. *Special Libraries*, 57 (1966) 111–13.

Wassermann, Paul. (ed.). *Catalog of museum publications and media*. 2nd edn. Gale (1980).

Waterman, Annette F. First step in planning the automation of a slide collection. *Art Documentation*, 8 (1989) 2, 61–65.

Waters, A. *Making and presenting slide shows*. Truro: Library Association branch and mobile group (1981).

Whitaker's books in print. London: Whitaker. 4 vols (1965 to date). Annual.

White, B. The SfB system: classification for the building industry. *Library Association Record*, 88 (1966) 428.

White, B. *Slide collections: a survey of their organisation in libraries in the fields of architecture, building and planning*. Edinburgh: The author (1967).

Williams, L. The slide collection of Westminster City libraries: fine arts library. In Aslib audio visual group. *Slides and sound recordings: their organisation and exploitation*. London: Aslib (1972). 47–49.

Wright, D. (comp.). *Directory of medical and health care libraries in the United Kingdom and Republic of Ireland*. London: Health and Welfare group of the Library Association. 8th edn (1992).

Wright, R.M. Arrangement and indexing. In Harrison, H.P. (ed.). *Picture Librarianship*. London: Library Association (1981). 131–49.

Writers' and artists' yearbook. London: A & C Black. Annual.

Appendices

In such a rapidly changing field as image database technology the following appendices can only be indicative. They represent a sample of the more prominent names from a much greater total of organizations, products and activities. Omission of any particular organization or product does not imply inferiority or irrelevance to the fields concerned.

For further information the reader is referred to the many directories which cover these areas, for example, Maher, Ann, ed. Software user's yearbook 1994. 4 vols. *VNU Business Publications.*

Appendix 1

Glossary

AIV	Advanced Interactive Video Disc
CAR	Computer Assisted Retrieval
CAV	Constant Angular Velocity
CD	Compact Disc
CD+G	Compact Disc plus Graphics
CD-DA	Compact Disc Digital Audio
CD-I	Compact Disc Interactive (Philips)
CD-MO	Compact Disc Magneto Optical
CD-R	Compact Disc Recordable
CD-ROM	Compact Disc Read Only Memory
CD-ROM XA	Compact Disc Read Only Memory Extended Architecture
CD-TMO	Compact Disc Thermo Magneto Optical
CD-V	Compact Disc Video
CD-WO	Compact Disc Write Once
CDTV	Commodore Dynamic Total Vision
CGA	Colour Graphics Array
CLV	Constant Linear Velocity
CRVdisc	Component Recording Videodisc (Sony)
DAT	Digital Audio Tape
DRAW	Direct Read After Write
DVI	Digital Video Interactive (Intel)
EGA	Enhanced Graphics Adaptor, 640×350 pixels
FSFM	Full Screen, Full Motion

gb	gigabyte
GUI	Graphical User Interface
HDTV	High Definition Television
ISDN	Integrated Services Digital Network
ISO	International Standardization Organization
JPEG	Joint Picture Experts Group
kb	kilobyte
mb	megabyte
MGA	Monochrome Graphics Array
MMC	Multimedia PC Marketing Council
MPEG	Motion Picture Experts Group
OMDR	Optical Memory Disc Recorder (Panasonic)
Pixel	Picture element
RLV	Recordable Laser Video Disc (Optical Disc Corporation)
SVGA	Super Video Graphics Array, 1024×768 pixels
VDU	Visual Display Unit
VGA	Video Graphics Array, 640×480 pixels.
WMRM	Write Many Read Many times
WORM	Write Once Read Many times
XGA	Extra Graphics Array, 1280×1024 pixels

Appendix 2

Some prominent general database packages which appear in the literature as being applied to picture and slide collection management

DataEase

Sapphire DataEase Ltd
1 Coventry Road
Ilford
Essex
IG1 4QR
(081) 554 0582

dBase IV

Ashton-Tate (UK) Ltd
Oaklands
1 Bath Road
Maidenhead
Berkshire
SL6 4UH
(0628) 33123

Microsoft Access

Microsoft Ltd
84 Caversham Road
Reading
Berkshire
RG1 8LP
(0734) 500741

Paradox

Borland International (UK) Ltd
8 Pavilions
Ruscombe Business Park
Twyford
Berkshire
RG10 9NN
(0734) 320022

Appendix 3

Specialist automated picture and/or slide management systems

This list covers software developed specifically to manage picture, photograph and slide collections of varying scale and sophistication.

ASHTON-KANE ASSOCIATES
(Picture Library System)
Westmead House
123 Westmead Road
Sutton
Surrey
SM1 4JH
(081) 770 1100

CRADOC CAPTIONWRITER
IRIS Audio Visual
Unit M
Forest Industrial Park
Forest Road
Hainault
Essex
IG6 3HL
(081) 559 8780

FIRST OPTION
(Image Folio software for picture libraries and archives)
Napier House
The Abbas Business Centre
Itchen Abbas
Hampshire
SO21 1BQ
(0962) 779794

G7 COMPUTER SERVICES
(A PLUS software for picture libraries)
Clapgate House
Broadcut
Wallington
Fareham
Hampshire
PO16 8ST
(0329) 828384

GEAC COMPUTER CORPORATION LTD
11 Allstate Parkway
Markham
Ontario
Canada
L3R 9T8
(416) 475 0525

GEAC COMPUTERS LTD
(ImagePower)
Hollywood Tower
Hollywood Lane
Cribbs Causeway
Bristol
BS10 7TW
(0272) 509 003

GOFER
Second Floor
843-845 Green Lanes
Winchmore Hill
London
N21 2RX
(081) 360 0144

INMAGIC PLUS
Soutron Ltd
Jerome House
Hallam Fields Road
Ilkeston
Derbyshire
DE7 4BH
(0602) 441664

JRM SOFTWARE LTD
(Library Index and Photo Tracking)
Sue Holt
Andil House
Court Street
Trowbridge
Wiltshire
BA14 8BR
(0225) 760251

LOGIC INFORMATION SYSTEMS LTD
191 Shoreditch High Street
London
E1 6HU
(071) 739 2941

MICROCHARM
(Photosoft)
David Picken
County Farm
Leicester Road
South Creake
Fakenham
Norfolk
NR21 9PW
(0328) 823209

MICROINFO LTD
PO Box 3
Omega Park
Alton
Hampshire
GU34 2PG
(0420) 86848

MUSEUMS DOCUMENTATION ASSOCIATION (MDA)
(MODES for Photographic Collections)
Lincoln House
347 Cherry Hinton Road
Cambridge
CB1 4DH
(0223) 242848

PHOTO LIBRARY MANAGEMENT SERVICES
Sandra Kinsler
2674 East Main St
Suite C-240
Ventura
CA 93003-2899

PHOTOFILE LIMITED
(Phototracer)
Unit 5
110 Coast Road
West Mersea
Colchester
Essex
CO5 8PA
(0206) 385 249

PHOTOMARKETING SYSTEMS LTD (PSL)
(Phototrack software)
Pages Green House
Wetheringsett
Stowemarket
Suffolk
IP14 5QA
(0728) 861 159

PROSOFT CONSULTANTS
10 Coates Gardens
Edinburgh
EH12 5LB
(031) 313 3776

UNIVERSITY OF LANCASTER LIBRARY
(LANSLIDE)
Ken Harrison
University of Lancaster
Bailrigg
Lancaster
LA1 4YH
(0524) 65201 Ext 2541

VISUAL RESOURCES MANAGEMENT SYSTEM (VRMS)
Slideware
PO Box 194
Sausalito
CA 94966
USA

WILLOWS GALLERY
(Compu-slide software package)
84 Lawrence Moorings
Sawbridgeworth
Hertfordshire
CM21 9PE
(0279) 722010

Appendix 4

Professional associations and other relevant bodies

This list includes bodies either with a direct specialized interest in image or slide management or with a more general information interest, but encompassing the management of pictorial information within a wider brief.

AMERICAN FILM AND VIDEO ASSOCIATION (AFVA)
920 Barnsdale Road
Suite 152
La Grange Park
Illinois 60525
USA

AMERICAN LIBRARY ASSOCIATION
50 E. Horon Street
Chicago
IL 60611
USA

AMERICAN MEDICAL ASSOCIATION
Council on Medical Education
515 North State Street
Chicago
IL 60610
USA

**ART LIBRARIES SOCIETY OF NORTH AMERICA
(ARLIS/NA)**
c/o Pamela J Parry
Executive Director
3900 East Timrod Street
Tucson
Arizona 85711
USA

ARLIS/NA Visual Resources Division
Christine Bunting
University of California
University Library
Santa Cruz
CA 95064

**ART LIBRARIES SOCIETY UK AND IRELAND (ARLIS/UK
AND IRELAND)**
Sonia French
Administrator
18 College Road
Bromsgrove
Worcestershire
B60 2NE

**ASSOCIATION FOR THE VISUAL ARTS IN IRELAND
(AVAIL)**
Elizabeth Kirwan
National Library of Ireland
Dublin
Ireland

ASSOCIATION OF AMERICAN MEDICAL COLLEGES
2450 N Street NW
Washington DC
20037-1126

ASSOCIATION OF FASHION, ADVERTISING AND EDITORIAL PHOTOGRAPHERS
9/10 Domingo Street
London
EC1Y 0TA
(071) 608 1441

ASSOCIATION OF ILLUSTRATORS
1 Colville Place
London
W1P 1HN
(071) 636 4100

BRITISH ASSOCIATION OF PICTURE LIBRARIES AND AGENCIES (BAPLA)
13 Woodberry Crescent
London
N10 1PJ
(081) 444 7913

BRITISH INSTITUTE OF PROFESSIONAL PHOTOGRAPHY
Fox Talbot House
2 Amwell End
Ware
Hertfordshire
SG12 9HN
(0920) 464011

BUREAU OF FREELANCE PHOTOGRAPHERS (BFP)
Focus House
497 Green Lanes
London
N13 4BP
(081) 882 3315/6

COLLEGE ART ASSOCIATION
275 Seventh Avenue
New York
NY 10001

GETTY ART HISTORY INFORMATION PROGRAMME
401 Wilshire Boulevard
Suite 1100
Santa Monica
CA 90401-1455
(310) 451-6366
USA

HEALTH SCIENCES COMMUNICATIONS ASSOCIATION
6105 Lindell Boulevard
St Louis
MO 63112
USA

INSTITUTE OF INFORMATION SCIENTISTS
UK Online User Group (UKOLUG)
44 Museum Street
London
WC1A 1LY

IVCA (INTERNATIONAL VISUAL COMMUNICATION ASSOCIATION)
5/6 Clipstone Street
London
W1P 7EB
(071) 580 0962/3

LIBRARY ASSOCIATION AUDIOVISUAL GROUP
Dr A. H. Thompson
The Coach House Frongog
Llanbadarn Fawr
Aberystwyth
SY23 3NN
Wales
(0970) 617322

LIBRARY INFORMATION TECHNOLOGY CENTRE (LITC)
South Bank Technopark
90 London Road
London
SE1 6LN
(071) 815 7872

**LIBRARY OF CONGRESS PRINTS AND PHOTOGRAPHS
DIVISION**
10 First St SE
Washington DC 20540
USA

MEDICAL LIBRARY ASSOCIATION
6 North Michigan Avenue
Suite 300
Chicago
Illinois
60602
USA

MUSEUMS ASSOCIATION
34 Bloomsbury Way
London
WC1A 2SA
(071) 431 0167

PHOTOGRAPHIC SOCIETY OF AMERICA
3000 United Founders Boulevard
Suite 103
Oklahoma City
OK 73112
USA

**PROFESSIONAL SPORTS PHOTOGRAPHERS
ASSOCIATION (PSPA)**
13 Woodberry Crescent
London
N10 1PJ
(081) 883 0083

ROYAL PHOTOGRAPHIC SOCIETY
The Octagon
Milsom Street
Bath
BA1 1DN
(0225) 626841

SOCIETY OF PICTURE RESEARCHERS AND EDITORS (SPREd)
BM Box 259
London
WC1N 3XX
(071) 581 1371

SPECIAL LIBRARIES ASSOCIATION
Kathryn Dorko
Manager Information Resources
1700 18th St NW
Washington DC 20009
USA

SPECIAL LIBRARIES ASSOCIATION PICTURE DIVISION
(SLA News Division)
Donna Scheeder (Chair)
Library of Congress
Congressional Reference Division
First & Independence Avenues
Washington DC 20540
USA

UNIVERSITY FILM AND VIDEO ASSOCIATION
7101 W80 Street
Los Angeles
CA 900045
USA

VISUAL RESOURCES ASSOCIATION (VRA)
Christina Updike
Visual Resources Curator
Art Department
James Madison University
Harrisonburg
Virginia 22807
USA

Appendix 5

Producers/developers/publishers of CD, multimedia technology, image databases or imaging systems

ACE COIN EQUIPMENT LTD
Stafford Park 6
Telford
TF3 3BQ
(0952) 293333

CD-ROM SYSTEMS (EUROPE) LTD
4 Lloyds Court
Manor Royal
Crawley
West Sussex
RH10 2XT
(0293) 525271

CHADWYCK-HEALEY LTD
Cambridge Place
Cambridge
CB2 1NR
(0223) 311479

DIGITHURST LTD
Newark Close
Royston
Hertfordshire
SG8 5HL
(0763) 242955

ELF PRESENTATION PRODUCTS
Unit 27
Hawthorn Trading Estate
Eastbourne
East Sussex
BN23 6QA
(0323) 647465

GRAVES EDUCATIONAL RESOURCES
Holly House
220 New London Road
Chelmsford
Essex
CM2 9BJ
(0245 283351)

IBM (UK) LTD
PO Box 41
North Harbour
Portsmouth
PO6 3AU
(0705) 321212

IBM
NATIONAL ENQUIRY CENTRE
(081) 995 1441

KODAK LTD
Kodak House
PO Box 66
Station Road
Hemel Hempstead
Hertfordshire
HP1 1JU
(0442) 61122

MICROSOFT
84 Caversham Road
Reading
Berkshire
RG1 8LP
(0734) 500741

PANASONIC UK
Kenmoor Road
Wakefield 41
Business Park
Wakefield
WF2 0XE
(0924) 821010

PHILIPS INTERACTIVE MEDIA (CONSUMER ELECTRONICS) LTD
City House
420-430 London Road
Croydon
Surrey
CR9 3QR
(081) 689 4444

PHOTOBASE LTD
(Livelink)
Trafalgar House
Grenville Place
Mill Hill
London NW7 3SA
(081) 906 4060

SILVER PLATTER INFORMATION LTD
10 Barley Mow Passage
Chiswick
London
W4 4PH
(081) 995 8242

SONY BROADCAST AND PROFESSIONAL UK
The Heights
Brooklands
Weybridge
Surrey
KT13 0XW
(0932) 816000

SONY TECHNICAL SERVICES
Viables
Jays Close
Basingstoke
Hampshire
RG22 4SB
(0256) 474011

VIDEOLOGIC LTD
Home Park Estate
Kings Langley
Hertfordshire
WD4 8LZ
(0923) 260 511

Appendix 6

Centres of activity in audio-visual and image management

ARTS COUNCIL OF GREAT BRITAIN
14 Great Peter Street
London
SW1P 3NQ
(071) 333 0100

AXIS (VISUAL ARTS EXCHANGE AND INFORMATION SERVICE)
Leeds Metropolitan University
Calverley Street
Leeds
LS1 3HE
(0532) 833125

BRIDGEMAN ART LIBRARY
19 Chepstow Road
London
W2 5BP
(071) 727 4065

BRITISH UNIVERSITIES FILM AND VIDEO COUNCIL
55 Greek Street
London
W1V 5LR
(071) 734 3687

BRITISH LIBRARY INFORMATION SCIENCES SERVICE (BLISS)
7 Ridgmount Street
London
WC1E 7AE
(071) 323 7688

CENTRE FOR IMAGE INFORMATION
Division of Learning Development
De Montfort University
The Gateway
Leicester
LE1 9EH
(0533) 551551

CENTRE FOR RESEARCH IN LIBRARY AND INFORMATION MANAGEMENT (CERLIM)
The Library
University of Central Lancashire
St Peter's Square
Preston
PR1 2HE
(0772) 892266

**CIMTECH
NATIONAL CENTRE FOR INFORMATION MEDIA AND TECHNOLOGY**
PO Box 109
College Lane
Hatfield
Hertfordshire
AL10 9AB

COURTAULD INSTITUTE OF ART
20 Portman Street
London W1H OBE
(071) 873 2742

HULTON PICTURE COMPANY
Unique House
21–31 Woodfield Road
London
W9 2BA
(071) 266 2662

LIBRARY INFORMATION TECHNOLOGY CENTRE (LITC)
South Bank Technopark
90 London Road
London
SE1 6LN
(071) 815 7872

MUSEUM DOCUMENTATION ASSOCIATION (MDA)
Lincoln House
347 Cherry Hinton Road
Cambridge
CB1 4DH
(0223) 833963

MUSEUMS AND GALLERIES COMMISSION
16 Queen Anne's Gate
London
SW1H 9AA

NATIONAL AUDIO VISUAL AIDS LIBRARY
George Building
Normal College
Bangor
Gwynedd
Wales
LL57 2PZ

NATIONAL AUDIOVISUAL CENTER (US)
8700 Edgeworth Drive
Capitol Heights
MD 20743-3701
USA

NATIONAL ART SLIDE LIBRARY
De Montfort University
The Gateway
Leicester
LE1 9BH
(0533) 577148 – Loans
(0533) 577036 – General enquiries

**NATIONAL CENTRE FOR FILM AND VIDEO
PRESENTATION (US)**
c/o American Film Institute
2021 N. Western Avenue
Los Angeles
CA 90027
USA

**NATIONAL COUNCIL FOR EDUCATIONAL
TECHNOLOGY (NCET)**
Sir William Lyons Road
Science Park
Coventry
CV4 7EZ

NATIONAL LIBRARY OF MEDICINE (US)
8600 Rockville Pike
Bethesda
Maryland
ND 20894
USA

ONLINE AUDIOVISUAL CATALOGUERS (US)
285 Sharp Road
Baton Rouge
LA 70815
USA

References

1 Background and trends in slide collection management

1 Lee, David J. Printed visual sources. In Higgins, G.L. (ed.). *Printed reference material*. 2nd edn. London: Library Association, 1984. pp. 563–87.

2 Lee. ibid. p. 577.

3 Allason-Jones, Lindsay. The case for BAPLA membership. *BAPLA Journal*. 1 (1994) 15.

4 Some of the earlier directories which include details of slide collections are:

Brink, A. (ed.). *The libraries, museums and art galleries yearbook 1978–79*. Cambridge: James Clarke, 1981.
British Association of Picture Libraries and Agencies BAPLA directory: a list of members, a subject index and practical guide for libraries and their users. London: BAPLA, 1984.
British Industrial and Scientific Film Association. *List of still picture libraries*. London: BISFA, 1981.
Buxton, I.R. (ed.). *Library resources in Yorkshire and Humberside*. London: Library Association, 1980.
Eakins, Rosemary. (ed.). *Picture sources UK*. London: Macdonald, 1985.
Evans, Hilary and Mary. *Picture researcher's handbook*. 4th edn. London: Van Nostrand Reinhold,
Guide to government departments and other libraries. 1984. 26th. edn. London: British Library, 1984.
Linton, W.D. (comp.). *Directory of medical and health care*

libraries in the UK and Republic of Ireland. 6th edn. London: Library Association, 1986.

Wall, J. (comp.). *Directory of British photographic collections.* London: Heinemann, 1977.

5   See:

Clawson, C.R. and Rankowski, C.A. Classification and cataloguing of slides using color photocopying. *Special Libraries.* 69 (1978) 281–85.

Evans, Grace E. et al. Image bearing catalog cards for photolibraries: an overview and a proposal. *Special Libraries.* 70 (1979) 11, 462–70.

6   Clark, David R. Semantic descriptors and maps of meaning for videodisc images. *Programmed Learning and Educational Technology.* 23, 1 (1986) 84.

Clark's figure is based on the average English word being six characters in length and a colour TV picture a little over half a megabyte of digital storage.

7   McKeown, Roy. *National directory of slide collections.* London: British Library, 1990. British Library information guide no. 12.

See also McKeown, Roy and Otter, Mary Edmunds. *National survey of slide collections.* London: British Library, 1989. British Library Research paper no. 67 and McKeown, Roy. Slides as information materials: the national survey of slide collections. *Audiovisual Librarian.* 16 (1990) 3, 127–31.

8   Davis, R. The professional status of slide curators. *Art Libraries Society News Sheet.* No. 55. (1985) p. 3.

9   Clark. op. cit. p. 85.

10   Harrison, H.P. (ed.). *Picture librarianship.* London: Library Association, 1981. p. 6.

11   Clawson and Rankowski. op. cit. p. 281.

12   Coulson, Anthony J. Picture libraries: a survey of the present situation and a look into the future. *Audiovisual Librarian.* 15 (1989) 99–102.

13   Thompson, A.H. Audiovisual materials. In Lea, P.W. (ed.). *Printed reference material.* 3rd edn. London: Library Association, 1990. p. 368.

14   For other definitions see:

Anglo-American cataloguing rules. 2nd edn. London: Library Association, 1978. p. 570.

Harrod, L.M. *The librarians' glossary.* 5th edn. London: Gower, 1984. p. 718.

Harrod. ibid. p. 787.

Shifrin, M. *Information in the school library: an introduction to the organisation of non-book materials.* London: Bingley, 1973. p. 113.

Bradfield, V.J. *Slide collections: a user requirement survey.* Leicester: Leicester Polytechnic, 1976. BLRD report no. 5309. p. 9.

British Standards Institution. *Specification for slides and film strips.* London: BSI, 1968. BS 1917.

15   Irvine, Betty Jo. *Slide libraries: a guide for academic institutions, museums, and special collections.* 2nd edn. Littleton, Colorado: Libraries Unlimited, 1979.

16   Hoort, Rebecca Miller. (ed.). Special issue: Professionalism. *Visual Resources.* 6 (1990) 4, 315–422.

17   Sutcliffe, G. S. *The management and exploitation of photographic slide collections in university teaching hospitals.* Unpublished M.Phil. thesis. Aberystwyth: University of Wales, 1989.

2   The literature of slide collection management
1   For standards see:

ARLIS/UK and EIRE. ARLIS working party on standards and guidelines. *Guidelines for art and design libraries: stock, planning, staffing and autonomy.* ARLIS/UK and EIRE, 1990.

Irvine, Betty Jo. (ed.). *Facilities standards for art libraries and visual resources collections.* Englewood, Colorado: Libraries unlimited, 1991.

The latter reference here is of more practical value as far as slides are concerned. Section 18 is devoted to slides and specifies figures for recommended standards and other useful figures e.g. 30 glass-bound slides weigh one pound, 350,000 slides weigh 5,266 kg without cabinets.

2   Schuller, Nancy Shelby. *Management for visual resources collections*. 2nd edn. Englewood, Colorado: Libraries Unlimited, 1989. p. ix.

3   Simons, W.W. and Tansey, L.C. *A slide classification system for the organisation and automatic indexing of interdisciplinary collections of slides and pictures*. Santa Cruz: University of California, 1970.

4   See: Bradfield, V.J. *Slide collections: a user requirement survey*. Leicester Polytechnic. 1976. BLRD report no. 5309.
Irvine, B.J. *Slide libraries: a guide for academic institutions, museums, and special collections*. 2nd edn. Littleton, Colorado: Libraries Unlimited, 1979.
Strohlein, A. *The management of 35mm medical slides*. New York: United Business Publications, 1975.

5   Freitag, W.M. and Irvine, B.J. Slides. In Grove, P.S. (ed.). *Non print media in academic libraries*. Chicago: American Library Association, 1975. pp. 105–07.

6   Irvine, B.J. *Slide libraries: a guide for academic institutions, museums and special collections*. 2nd edn. Littleton, Colorado: Libraries Unlimited, 1979. pp. 31–34.

7   Bradfield, V.J. *Slide collections: a user requirement survey*. Leicester: Leicester Polytechnic, 1976. BLRD report no. 5309. pp. 14–18.

8   Dewey, Melvil. Picture libraries. *Public Libraries*. 11 (1906) 10.

9   Irvine, B.J. Slide collections in art libraries. *College and Research Libraries*. 30 (1969) 443–45.
Irvine, B.J. Slide classification: a historical survey. *College and Research Libraries*. 32 (1971) 23–30.
Irvine, B.J. Organisation and management of art slide collections. *Library Trends*. 23 (1975) 401–16.
Irvine, B.J. *Slide libraries: a guide for academic institutions, museums, and special collections*. 2nd edn. Littleton, Colorado: Libraries Unlimited, 1979.

10   Gunther, Alfred. Slides in documentation. *Unesco Bulletin for Libraries*. 17 (1963) 157–63.

11   Irvine, B.J. Slide classification: a historical survey. *College and Research Libraries*. 32 (1971) 25.

12   ibid. p. 25.
13   The following guides which had their origin in the Mid-America College Art Association (MACAA) became the responsibility of the Visual Resources Association. Some of the titles were updated and expanded to form substantial works.

Collins, Eleanor (ed.). *Guide for collections without curators*.

Kuehn, Rosemary and Richardson, Zelda. *Guide to copy photography for visual resource collections*.

Schuller, Nancy (ed.). *Guide to management of visual resources collections*.

Scott, Gillian (ed.). *Guide to equipment for slide maintenance and viewing*.

Tamulonis, Susan (ed.). *Guide to photograph collections*.

The Association also carried out groundwork in the following areas: Guide to computer programs for visual resources collections; Architectural slide collections; Classification and cataloguing of slides and a statement of slide standards.

14   Diamond, R. *The development of a retrieval system for 35mm slides utilised in art and humanities instruction*. Fredonia, New York: State University College of New York at Fredonia, 1969.

Diamond, R. A retrieval system for 35mm slides utilised in art and humanities instruction. In Grove, P.S. and Clement, E.G. (eds). *Bibliographical control of non print media*. Chicago: American Library Association, 1972. pp. 346–59.

15   Simons, W.W. and Tansey, L.C. *A slide classification system for the organisation and automatic indexing of interdisciplinary collections of slides and pictures*. Santa Cruz: University of California, 1970.

Simons, W.W. Development of a universal classification system for two-by-two inch slide collections. In Grove, P.S. and Clement, E.G. (eds). *Bibliographic control of nonprint media*. Chicago: American Library Association, 1972. pp. 360–73.

Tansey, L. Classification of research photographs and slides. *Library Trends*. 23 (1975) 417–26.

Tansey, L. and Simons, W. The computer at Santa Cruz: slide classification with automated cross-indexing. *Picturescope*. 18 (1979) 64–75.

16   Wright, R.M. Arrangement and indexing. In Harrison, H.P. (ed.). *Picture Librarianship*. London: Library Association, 1981. p. 136–39.

17   Krause, M.G. Intellectual problems of indexing picture collections. *Audiovisual Librarian*. 14 (1988) 73–81.

18   Strohlein, A. *The management of 35mm medical slides*. New York: United Business Publications, 1975.

19   Hedley, A.J. and Morton, R. The clinical slide library: a valuable learning resource in continuing medical education. *Medical and Biological Illustration*. 26 (1976) 203–07.

20   Barker, V.F. and Harden, R. *The storage and retrieval of 35mm slides*. Dundee: Association for the Study of Medical Education, 1980. Medical Education Booklet no. 11.

21   Tabour, R.B. The use of 35mm transparencies in the National Health Service. In Aslib audio visual group. *Slides and sound recordings: their organisation and exploitation*. London: Aslib, 1972. pp. 56–63.

22   McKenna, M. Regional av services. In Tabour, R.B. (ed.). *Libraries for health: the Wessex experience*. Southampton: Wessex Regional Library and Information Service, 1978. pp. 115–16.

23   Delaurier, Nancy. Visual resources: the state of the art. *Art Libraries Journal*. 7 (1982) 3, 7–21.

24   ibid. p. 10.

25   Delaurier. op. cit. p. 12.

26   Delaurier. op. cit. p. 13.

27   Davis, R. The professional status of slide curators. *Art Libraries Society News Sheet*. No. 55. (1985) p. 3.

28   Hoort, Rebecca Miller. General introduction. *Visual Resources*. 6 (1990) 4, 316–19.

29   Gilson, C.C. and Collins, J.M. Use of a microcomputer in a department of medical illustration for retrieval of clinical teaching slides. *Journal of Audiovisual Media in medicine*. 5 (1982) 130–34.

30   Markey, K. Visual art resources and computers: slide collec-

tions. In Williams, M.E. (ed.). *Annual review of information science and technology.* Vol 19. New York: Knowledge Industry Publications, Inc. 1984. pp. 282–84.

31   Harrison, K. and Clark, W.R. LANSLIDE – the development of a system for managing a slide collection at the University of Lancaster Library. *Program.* 22 (1988) 4, 365–77.
Clark, W.R. and Harrison, K. LANSLIDE: the automation of the University of Lancaster Library's slide collection. *Audiovisual Librarian.* 14 (1988) 4, 196–200.

32   Waterman, Annette F. First steps in planning the automation of a slide collection. *Art Documentation.* 8 (1989) 2, 61–65.

33   Collins, Donna Lacey. A slide library database using the Apple Macintosh plus system. *Visual Resources* V (1988) 2, 135–50.

34   ibid. p. 143.

35   Collins op. cit. p. 147.

36   Pearman, Sara Jane. An opinion: mumblings of a slide librarian. *Art Documentation.* 7 (1988) 4, 145–46.

37   Snow, Maryly. Visual depictions and the use of MARC: a view from the trenches of slide librarianship. *Art Documentation.* 8 (1989) 186–87 and 189–90.

38   Bakewell, Elisabeth and Schmitt, Marilyn. *Object, image, inquiry: the art historian at work.* Santa Monica: J. Paul Getty Trust, 1988.
Murray, P. Some problems of an art historian in a library. *ARLIS Newsletter.* (1975) 23, pp. 4–7.
Rhyne, Charles S. A slide collection of Constable's paintings: The art historian's need for visual documentation. *Visual Resources.* 4 (1987) 1, 51–70.

39   See entry for 'Iconography and iconology' in *Encyclopedia of World Art.* 15 vols. New York: McGraw-Hill, 1968.

40   Markey, Karen. *Subject access to visual resources collections.* New York: Greenwood, 1986.

41   Panofsky, Erwin. *Studies in iconology.* New York: Harper and Row, 1962.
Panofsky, Erwin. *Meaning in the Visual Arts.* New York: Doubleday Anchor Books, 1955.

42   Barnett, Patricia J. The art and architecture thesaurus as a faceted MARC format. *Visual Resources.* 4 (1987) 247–59.

43   Small, Jocelyn Penny. Retrieving images verbally. *Library Hi Tech.* 9 (1991) 1, 51–60.

44   Roddy, Kevin. Subject access to visual resources. *Library Hi Tech.* 9 (1991) 1, 45–49.

45   Roberts, Helen E. The visual document. *Art Libraries Journal.* 13 (1988) 2, 5–8.

46   Couprie, L.D. Iconclass: an iconographic classification system. Art Libraries Journal. 8 (1983) 2, 32–49.

47   Brumm, E.K. Optical disc technology for information management. In Williams, M.E. (ed.). *Annual review of information science and technology.* Vol. 26 (1991) pp. 197–240.

48   Danziger, Pamela N. Picture databases: a practical approach to picture retrieval. *Database.* 13 (1990) 4, 13–17.

49   Morton, Richard. The image database: pictures and computers. *Journal of Audiovisual Media in Medicine.* 15 (1992) 2, 54–56.

50   Rowland, Melanie and Seeley, Maureen. Image databases – the facts of life. *Audiovisual Librarian* 17 (1991) 4, 217–20.

51   Ester, Michael. Image quality and viewer perception. *Visual Resources.* 7 (1991) 4, 327–52.

52   For example, Pring, Isobel. (ed.). IMAGE '89: *The international meeting on museums and art galleries image databases.* London: IMAGE, 1990.

3   Slide aquisitions

1   McKeown, Roy. The Centre for Image Information: the shape of things to come. *Art Libraries Journal.* 18 (1993) 3, 28–31.

2   Pinion, Catherine F. Preserving our audiovisual heritage: a national and international challenge. *Audiovisual Librarian.* 19 (1993) 3, 205–19.

3   Terris, Olwen. AVANCE: a multimedia database. *Audiovisual Librarian.* 16 (1990) 3, 112–15.

4   The technical preparation of slides as stock items

1   Strohlein, A. *The management of 35mm medical slides.* New York: United Business Publications, 1975. p. 81.

2　Kodak. *Storage and care of Kodak photographic materials before and after processing*. Hemel Hempstead: Kodak, 1992.
3　Sundt, Christine L. *Conservation practices for slide and photograph collections*. VRA Special Bulletin No 3.: Visual Resources Association, 1989.

5　Slide retrieval
1　Foskett, A.C. *The subject approach to information* 4th edn. London: Bingley, 1982.
2　Dewey, Melvil. *Dewey decimal classification and relative index*. 20th edn. Albany, New York: Forest Press. 4 vols.
3　*Universal Decimal Classification (UDC)* BS 1000. British Standards Institution, 1958–
4　Austin, D. *Preserved Context Indexing System* PRECIS. London: BNB.
5　Robinson, C.D. Indexing nonbook materials by PRECIS. In Wellish, H.H. *The PRECIS indexing system: principles, applications and prospects*. H.W. Wilson, 1977. pp. 169–74.
6　Wright, R.M. Arrangement and indexing. In Harrison, H.P. (ed.). *Picture Librarianship*. London: Library Association, 1981. p. 136–39.
7　CI/SfB – International Council for Building Research Studies and Documentation (CIB). Samarbetskommitten for Byggnadsfragor (SfB).
8　For some theoretical and practical discussion see:

Diamond, R. *The development of a retrieval system for 35mm slides utilised in art and humanities instruction*. Fredonia, New York: State University College of New York at Fredonia, 1969.
Diamond, R. A retrieval system for 35mm slides utilised in art and humanities instruction. In Grove, P.S. and Clement, E.G. (eds). *Bibliographical control of nonprint media*. Chicago: American Library Association, 1972. pp. 346–59.
Krause, M.G. Intellectual problems of indexing picture collections. *Audiovisual librarian*. 14 (1988) 73–81.
Simons, W.W. and Tansey, L.C. *A slide classification system for the organisation and automatic indexing of interdisciplinary col-*

lections of slides and pictures. Santa Cruz: University of California, 1970.

Wright, R.M. Arrangement and indexing. In Harrison, H.P. (ed.). *Picture librarianship*. London: Library Association, 1981, p. 131–49.

6 Commercially available slide management and retrieval packages

1 Current issues of *VRA Bulletin* contain useful information and reports of the application of 'Dataease' to slide library management. Great benefits can be gained by user groups communicating their developments in this way, reducing the duplication of effort by isolated individuals.

7 Medical slide collections

1 The complexity of the levels of meaning and indexing inherent in visual arts images is well covered in a work of excellent clarity by Markey: Markey, Karen. *Subject access to visual resources collections*. New York and London: Greenwood Press, 1986.

2 Askham, David. *Photo libraries and agencies*. London: BFP Books, 1990.

3 List, David. *Audiovisual Librarian*. 17 (1991) 1, 53–54.

4 *The Journal of Audiovisual Media in Medicine*. Guildford: Butterworth-Heinemann (1976 to date). Quarterly.

5 Brophy, Peter. *Art Libraries Journal*. 16 (1991) 2, 33–35. Review of ARLIS/UK & Eire. *Guidelines for art and design libraries: stock, planning and autonomy*. ARLIS, 1990.

6 Williams, A.R. Victorian clinical photography. *Journal of Audiovisual Media in Medicine*. 5 (1982) 3, 100–03.

7 Hedley, A.J. and Morton, R. The clinical slide library: a valuable learning resource in continuing medical education. Medical and Biological Illustration. 26 (1976) 203–04.

8 Simons, W.W. and Tansey, L.C. *A slide classification system for the organisation and automatic indexing of interdisciplinary collections of slides and pictures*. Santa Cruz: University of California, 1970.

9 Strohlein, A. *The management of 35mm medical slides*. New York: United Business Publications, 1975. pp. 55–72.

10 Cilliers, J.M. Organisation of a slide collection in a medical library. *Medical Library Association Bulletin*. 69 (1981) 330–33.

11 Barker, V.F. and Harden, R.M. *The storage and retrieval of 35mm slides*. Dundee: Association for the Study of Medical Education, 1980. Medical Education Booklet no. 11. Reprinted in *Medical Education*. 14 (1980) 59–71.

12 Hedley, A.J. and Morton, R. The clinical slide library: a valuable learning resource in continuing medical education. *Medical and Biological Illustration*. 26 (1976) 203–07.

13 For work on manual post co-ordinate indexing, feature cards, or optical coincidence techniques in the medical field see also:
Harden, R.M. Indexing audiovisual aids on a feature card system. *Medical and Biological Illustration*. 18 (1968) 263.
Harden, R.M. et al. Punched feature card retrieval systems in clinical research. *British Journal of Hospital Medicine*. 13 (1975) 195.
Such techniques are still useful for use with small personal collections of slides where computers are not an option and in visualising some of the processes which automated methods now carry out so rapidly.

8   Optical disc systems and the slide

1 Clark, David R. The creation of a scholarly image databank. In Pring, I. (ed.). *IMAGE '89: The International Meeting on Museums and Art Galleries Image Databases. Proceedings of the IMAGE meeting held at The University of London Audio-Visual Centre, UK. 18–20 May 1989*. London: IMAGE, 1990.

2 Gartner, Richard. Digitising the Bodleian? *Audiovisual Librarian*. 19 (1993) 3, 220–23.

3 Godfrey, J. The visual imagery used in the teaching of Art and Design: problems of acquisition for the slide librarian. *Audiovisual Librarian*. 17 (1991) 2, 90–94.

4 Kemp, Martin. The making of slides from illustrations in books, periodicals etc. *Art Historians bulletin*. 35 (1991) p. 32.

5 Duffield, Rachel. Proposals for a slide library licensing scheme. *Audiovisual Librarian*. 19 (1993) 4, 285–86.

6 Philip, G. ISDN: an emerging electronic highway for busi-

ness data communication. *Journal of Information Science.* 19 (1993) 4, 279–89.

7　Wall, R.A. *Copyright made easier*. London: Aslib. 1993.

8　Ester, Michael. Image quality and viewer perception. *Visual Resources.* 7 (1991) 4, 327–52.

9　Eccles, David and Romans, Gary. High definition vs high resolution displays: what sort of image quality? *Advanced Imaging*. Sept. 1992. 16–20, 81.

Index